WINNING WITH WALL STREET

WINNING WITH WALL STREET

A TRADER'S GUIDE TO FINANCIAL FREEDOM

LEWIS DANIELS

WILEY

This edition first published 2025

Registered Office(s)
John Wiley & Sons, Inc., 111 River Street, Hoboken, NJ 07030, USA
John Wiley & Sons Ltd, The Atrium, Southern Gate, Chichester, West Sussex, PO19 8SQ, UK

Editorial Office
The Atrium, Southern Gate, Chichester, West Sussex, PO19 8SQ, UK

For details of our global editorial offices, customer services, and more information about Wiley products visit us at www.wiley.com.

Library of Congress Cataloging-in-Publication Data Is Available:

ISBN 9781394285037 (Paperback)
ISBN 9781394285051 (ePDF)
ISBN 9781394285044 (ePub)

Cover Design: Jon Boylan
Cover Images: © martinspurny/Getty Images,
© Kaspars Grinvalds/Adobe Stock Photos,
© mudasar/Adobe Stock Photos
Author Photo: Courtesy of Lewis Daniels

SKY10085638_092224

For my wife Angharad and my son Zack.
Everything I do and continue to do is for you.
I love you x

CONTENTS

FOREWORD

I've always been interested in trading. The glamour of Wall Street seemed captivating to me, but I never thought it was accessible to the public, to the average Joe. I didn't think you could trade unless you were part of the elite club, working for a bank or physically on the trading floors.

Even if by chance you could get in on the action, I thought Wall Street would take your money, chew you up and spit you out the second you placed a trade! How can you compete with the big boys? The institutions? The money makers?

This book actually helps you do just that! It gives you the means to be on the winning side!

Needless to say, I was amazed to discover my own husband had been trading since the age of 15! How was that possible?

The image of him on his pushbike cycling to his little local bank still makes me laugh, especially when I compare it to nowadays, when he's placing trades on his phone poolside! The accessibility of trading has evolved no end. Today, anyone can trade if they want; it doesn't matter how old you are, what profession you have or had, or how much money you do or don't have. It's all doable, and even more so when you're given an insight into how it all fits together.

Knowledge is key.

Without understanding the charts, trading is dangerous and Wall Street will beat you. Managing your risk is paramount! I'm mathematically minded but incredibly emotional! That's why I've been daunted by trading. How could I eliminate the emotion?

The answer is to apply logic and understanding. Statistically speaking, on a simple 3:1 profit ratio, you can be 70% wrong and still walk away winning. This is exciting, and that's why I'm so impressed with this book. Lewis has made me see trading in a different light. I don't want to undermine the years of work, dedication and trial and error that have got us to this point (I've lived it! Been beside him for the journey) but, after reading this book, it seems—dare I say—'easy', or at least achievable! It finally all makes sense. I could trade, too!

It's evident Lewis has a gift. An incredible talent for understanding the charts and being able to see the levels and patterns they hold with such accuracy. All his Discord members will agree; he has helped so many all over the world transform their trading style and shown them a different viewpoint.

Habit/instinct/practice, call it what you like, it's clear that he can see what many struggle to grasp.

His calls are repeatedly to the pip; it's impressive.

Hence, breaking down the logic behind what he sees into simple steps, like he has in this book, enables so many other traders the possibility to be successful.

Thank you for getting his book; I wish you all the best in your trading.

Enjoy what's to come!

—Angharad Daniels MA

PREFACE

I am Lewis Daniels, better known in the trading community as Mayfair Ventures.

I am also the author of *Master the Art of Trading.*

Many of you would know me for calling every significant Bitcoin move over the last couple of years with great success. I got lucky with an early entry; watching the transition of an asset class unfold in real time has been amazing.

This image shows each immutable call on Bitcoin.

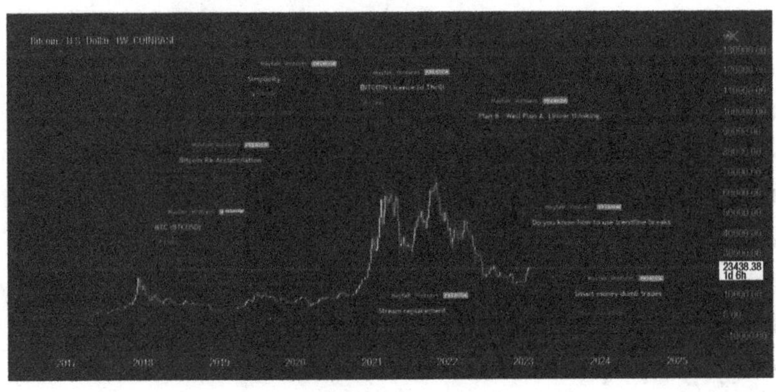

If you don't know me or haven't followed me, you might not know that I have been a trader for a long time; it all started when I was 15, on a school trip to Wall Street from Wales. Looking back, this was a big deal. The history trip was to learn about the 1929 Wall Street Crash.

Going and seeing the exchange in New York was an incredible opportunity. It is also one of the main reasons behind the book's title. For me, it's where it all began.

At age 15, I would take my pushbike to the bank and get the branch manager to phone the broker if the prices were near the same as the newspaper I would buy. In other words, purchase yesterday's prices tomorrow.

As the years passed, I tried my hand at all kinds of tradable instruments, from penny stocks to commodities, blue chips and forex. I bought my first Bitcoin in 2011.

As the internet became a factor, forex became the weapon of choice. It seemed even more exciting and didn't seem to shut like most 9-to-5 stocks.

In 2012 I set up a forex education business, running in parallel with several other businesses, but I always kept my hand in the trading world.

When the COVID-19 pandemic struck, I picked up trading full time again. There was a new wave of 'influencers' on YouTube and other social media platforms. Most have little to no experience yet millions of followers. It seemed so sad that there are enough ways to lose money trading; taking the wrong advice shouldn't be another one. These people make their money not by calling the market; they advertise a lavish lifestyle and sucker an audience with affiliate links and sign-up bonuses, with the majority of their income coming from YouTube views.

For this reason, I partnered up with Paul Varcoe and launched what is now known as the Mayfair Method, our Discord services—no broker affiliate shilling, just pure education.

In Discord we cover so many different topics but it became clear that by showing my unique method, the reasoning behind what I see and why, so many have benefitted from this different vantage point. Applying simple logic is the key!

My first book, *Master the Art of Trading*, touched on many aspects in trading but there is so much more we could cover. Hence, *Winning with Wall Street* gives you the next level.

I delve further into the Mayfair trading method style, although this book is more advanced (if you don't understand the fundamentals of trading, it will be harder to grasp).

This book takes you on a journey and breaks down the complexity of the charts to make them easier to translate and help you understand what you are looking for to become successful.

Mayfair Method Discord server can be accessed at: https://discord.gg/5t3w47raHe

ACKNOWLEDGEMENTS

I want to thank my wife for all her help with everything; I want to thank our incredible Discord community and most of all, my son Zack, as I wouldn't be writing books if it wasn't for him.

I also want to thank my history teacher. In all fairness it's because of him I began trading, so thank you for that New York trip! The trip that inspired the title.

Thanks to Gemma Valler at Wiley for everything she did to get the book published.

And, finally, to thank my business partner Paul Varcoe. I don't think I would have gone back into educational content if it wasn't for him.

INTRODUCTION

In the labyrinthine world of trading, where complexity often reigns supreme, a persistent struggle plagues the minds of traders who have traversed the terrain of countless courses and books.

If you find yourself amidst the disillusioned, having tried various methodologies, absorbed the jargon-laden tomes and waded through opinionated narratives that left you more confused than enlightened, fear not.

This book is not just another addition to the cacophony of trading literature; it is a beacon of clarity in a sea of complexity.

I often see people use 15 indicators on their charts, looking at hundreds of instruments on smaller timeframes—none of these things help you make money!

It is an assumption that the more technical you get, the easier it is to win. Often, it's more like 'All the gear, yet no idea'.

If there was a magic Artificial Intelligence tool or bot you could use to automate your trading, making you millions while you sleep, then the world would be empty of doctors, lawyers and accountants. They would all be professional traders!

People often fall prey to the misconception that becoming a professional trader can be achieved swiftly, perhaps by watching a single tutorial or purchasing an automated bot. In contrast, the demanding and rigorous journey of becoming a lawyer entails years of dedicated study and formal education. Why would trading professionally be any different?

In this book, I aim to provide you with comprehensive information on identifying liquidity and leveraging it to your advantage, without requiring an extensive university education.

In my first book, *Master the Art of Trading*, I covered in-depth details of some trading greats, including Elliott Wave Theory, Wyckoff schematics and Fibonacci techniques.

Winning with Wall Street will now take you behind the scenes. . . .

CHAPTER 1

RECAP FROM *MASTER THE ART OF TRADING*

'Every battle is won or lost before it's ever fought.'

—Sun Tzu

https://vocal.media/motivation/quotes-about-fights

In my first book I gave an insightful overview for novice traders through to intermediate, to simplify their trading. I tried to cover everything from psychology to technical analysis and why patience and discipline are critical to becoming a successful trader.

The book covered several techniques and styles of analysis and why combining such tools can create a significant edge. Unfortunately, newer traders are looking for a silver bullet, and any learning seems too much like hard work. But just like many other professions, trading takes time to learn and even longer to master. After more than two decades of studying various trading books and continuously learning, trading and educating others, I've consolidated this wealth of knowledge, ensuring that readers can access a comprehensive resource without investing the same significant amount of time.

Understanding risk is the key factor, and developing a bias is crucial. Combining these two elements is paramount to creating a successful risk management technique. Avoid get-rich-quick schemes and influencers who claim the ability to make you rich overnight!

A little common sense, mixed with sound risk management and the techniques taught in the book, will get you on the right path.

Now, take it to the next level!

This is the sole purpose of this second book.

Unfortunately, the majority of people these days treat trading like playing the lottery. People seem to think it's a strike-it-rich, one-hit type of tool. A doctor doesn't make it in his field by doing one operation, just like a Formula One driver—you need to keep winning to stay at the top.

In this book I aim to take you from an intermediate to an advanced trader. The book will be enough to keep you profiting from the market again and again.

Trading has evolved into a complex art form, where success demands a comprehensive understanding of market dynamics and precise analytical tools. Volume profiles and footprint analysis are potent methods for gaining unique insights into market behaviour; they can also be combined with the techniques discussed in *Master the Art of Trading*, from Elliott Wave Theory to Wyckoff analysis. It's not as simple as knowing the techniques; it is understanding when and where *not* to use them.

One of the critical factors of volume trading is knowing the participants.

Compared to many other books available, I have no intention of covering the basics here. If you don't know what a trendline or a moving average is, put this book down and learn from babypips.com, or read my first book, *Master the Art of Trading*, and then come back and read this one!

When trading using volume techniques, it's essential to understand the collective actions of market participants. Traders, investors, institutions and algorithms contribute to the constantly shifting market tides. Based on varying strategies, expectations and emotions, their decisions drive price movements.

Volume is a crucial aspect of market data; it represents the number of shares or contracts traded. It acts as a barometer of market activity and intensity, providing valuable insights into the strength and validity of price movements. So understanding volume patterns can help traders anticipate potential shifts in market sentiment.

I have carefully thought and mapped out each chapter here so you can advance quickly into understanding why volume will be helpful and how you can make it the newest addition to your trading strategy. Knowing when to apply volume tools and how to use these techniques, not just on the charts but at the right time, is the most significant factor; most people get this wrong! Many apply volume everywhere, overcomplicating the situation with countless indicators and unnecessary information, making it difficult to decipher the charts. I intend to help you look at a naked chart and instinctively grasp the fundamental message it portrays.

Let's begin.

CHAPTER 2
PSYCHOLOGY

'I believe in analysis and not forecasting.'

—Nicolas Darvas

https://realtrading.com/trading-blog/analyze-avoid-forecasting/

To be honest, this chapter was an afterthought. But on reading through my manuscript, I found it an essential piece of the puzzle. I could simply refer back to *Master the Art of Trading*, where I covered psychology in some depth. However, this time it's different.

You have probably come to this book through a number of channels. One, you know me, follow me or read the first book. Two, you have tried other literature or courses and still struggle.

This will mean you have built up emotions you might not realise, but they are emotions you have accumulated from your frustration over a long period. You think you have a bias towards a particular instrument or a certain indicator you have grown fond of. This causes hidden anxiety and without knowing it, it's this that starts you on the emotional rollercoaster.

I can also tell you that shaking these emotions is crucial for future performance.

Let me walk you through it.

Let's say you lose a trade; you start to get angry at yourself and then get angry at the market. This is where you begin to justify your setup—everything from the entry to the stop loss, lot size, etc. You can't figure out why it went against you.

Then what? Straight after, later that day or even tomorrow, you go into full-scale revenge mode!

You lose again, and this leads to creating a loop of self-criticism.

During winning periods, you feel like your strategy, indicator and instrument of choice are the best thing ever—until they are not.

Let me take this further: you make mistakes you deem silly or little. You then struggle to relax; you have a shorter fuse than usual—you are angry with the world! But it doesn't stop there; you draw lines on the chart and sit in front of the screen watching the price go from your stop loss seemingly straight to your take profit target!

Am I right? Just a little bit?

I bet you struggle to relax and then experience sleep issues.

You see, these are normal human emotions; we feel them when we lose, if our car has been bumped or a family pet dies. We are human, after all.

Losing money might trigger other emotions you don't want to admit to. You might feel like a failure, confused (your system worked in the last trade) or afraid of reading social media or talking to family and friends. You feel lost or alone.

Psychology also plays a significant role at the other end of the scale: you win a trade, a second, a third and you feel invincible—until you are not!

How about this one?

If you watch some YouTube videos or read an article, you tend to overconsume data by trying to learn more and more without fully absorbing it or understanding what to take from it.

I could go and write an entire book on trading psychology. I've been there, done that and bought the T-shirt, as they say. You have to go back to basics, almost unlearn what you have learned, from indicators to emotions. As a trader, you must practically become robotic when executing your strategy. In other words, take the feelings away.

I can safely say that.

Occasionally, your market intuition is accurate, but such instances are rare. More frequently, you grapple with varying levels of confusion, overthinking and second-guessing your decisions. Your mind is crowded with numerous ideas and perspectives, leading to frustration and stress. Taking a few days off may offer a short-term respite, but the issue persists, repeatedly resurfacing. I will not try to fix these issues for you in terms of psychology; instead, I will show you techniques that will alleviate the cause.

The apparent problem is stress, so you assume it's a mental game problem. But this is only half true.

Every trader will feel greed or confidence, frustration and fear—often anger. Like I said, we are human, after all. When you believe in the process and have tested the results, limit your screen time, indicators and instruments. You will realise it wasn't a mental game issue; it was knowing the game well enough to play it correctly.

Trading is exciting, but it's also a scary journey. It can be incredibly lonely.

It's not for the faint-hearted.

If you don't understand what you're doing, then it's simply gambling, and my advice would be that if you haven't got the time or interest to dedicate to understanding it, then don't even bother.

Instead, go to Las Vegas, have an epic holiday, drink Bellinis at the Bellagio, see the O show and win or lose, you'll have had fun along the way!

Trading is no fun if you don't win, it's no fun if you lose all the time and it's petrifying if you rely on trading to pay your bills. It messes with your mind and your psychology if you're down—the desperation and fear overrule sound logic. And when you're on a winning streak, greed can take over and easily wipe you out. So risk management is crucial to successful trading, as is understanding what to look for and being on the winning side!

CHAPTER 3

TYPES OF VOLUME

'If you can learn to create a state of mind that's not affected by the market's behavior, the struggle will cease to exist.'

—Mark Douglas

https://traderlion.com/quotes/mark-douglas-quotes/

Let's kick off this book with a few essential pointers in terms of the types of volume available. You may have heard of some of these; more often than not, you might only think of volume as traditional bars on the bottom of a chart's X-axis.

After covering a lot of these types and styles of volume tools in *Master the Art of Trading*, I didn't want to go as deep in this book as it's not necessarily needed once you train your eyes.

I wrote this book to be like we're just having a friendly chat, straight to the point. No fluff or extra nonsense. I want you to get it; feel free to go back and read a page or a chapter as many times as you want.

So, let's jump straight in!

The most common type of volume, I would say, is

Volume Bars. Volume Bars/Volume Candles are the most basic and commonly used volume tools. Instead of displaying the price data on the charts, also incorporate volume data. Each bar or candle on the chart represents a specific period (e.g., one minute, one hour, one day) and the height or width of the bar/candle represents the volume traded during that period. Volume bars/candles help traders visualise the trading activity at different price levels and timeframes.

As you can see in the box on the chart's X-axis, each volume bar represents the volume of each corresponding candlestick above.

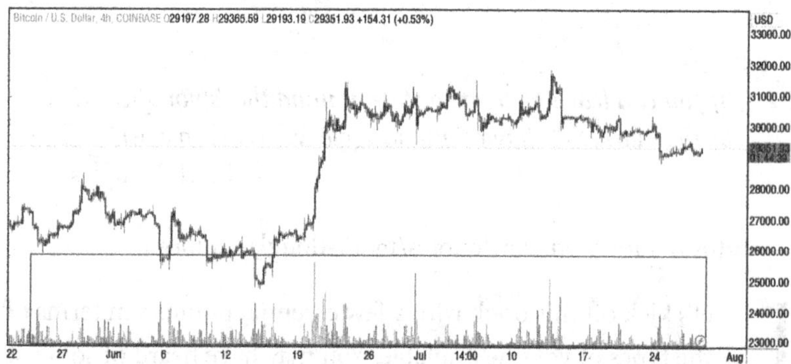

Volume Profile. Volume Profile is a powerful tool that displays the volume traded at different price levels over a specific period. It creates a histogram on the chart, illustrating the volume concentration at various price levels. Traders can identify significant support and resistance levels and areas of high liquidity and potential trading opportunities.

As you can see from this chart, the histogram is added from the swing low to the swing high.

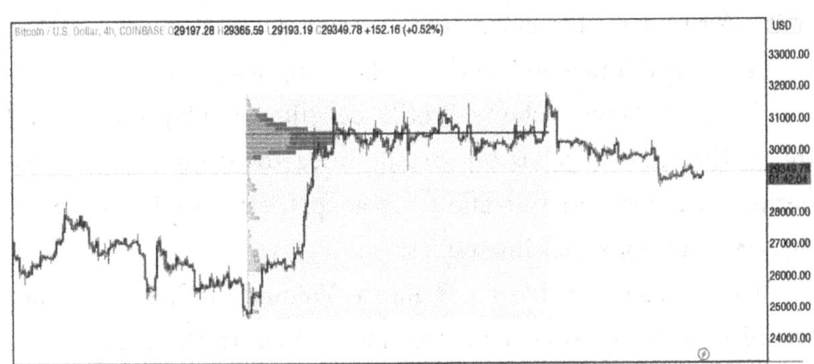

There are several variations of this type of histogram-related volume profile. These include

Fixed Range Volume Profile. Fixed Range Volume Profile is a specific approach within Volume Profile trading that focuses on analysing the volume traded within a fixed price range rather than a particular period. Instead of using a specified time interval (e.g., one day or one hour), traders using a Fixed Range Volume Profile look at the volume traded within a predetermined price range, irrespective of the time it took to form.

Creating a Fixed Range Volume Profile involves selecting a specific price range on the price chart and measuring the volume traded within that range. Traders often use horizontal lines to define the range, marking the high and low prices for the period they want to analyse.

The main advantage of using a Fixed Range Volume Profile is that it can provide valuable insights into short-term price action and market sentiment within a particular price bracket. It helps identify significant trading activity and liquidity areas, which can act as support or resistance levels. These levels can become crucial reference points for traders, influencing their trading decisions, such as where to enter or exit trades and where to place stop-loss orders.

A Fixed Range Volume Profile benefits intraday traders and those who want to focus on specific price zones instead of whole periods. It allows traders to effectively adapt their analysis to different market conditions and timeframes.

Traders can combine Fixed Range Volume Profiles with other technical analysis tools to enhance their trading strategies. For example, they may use traditional support and resistance levels, trendlines or moving averages with the volume profile analysis to gain a more comprehensive market view.

In addition to Fixed Range Volume Profiles, you also have Visible Range; as the name suggests, this paints a histogram that relates to the price visible on the chart.

As you can see in this image, it shows the histogram on the right side of the chart and gives the profile of the candlesticks visible on the screen.

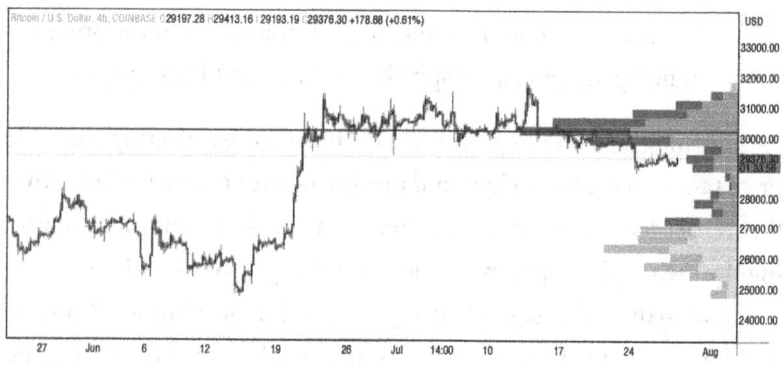

Both Fixed Range and Visible Range Volume Profiles are valuable tools for traders, and each has its benefits depending on the trader's objectives and trading style.

Benefits of Fixed Range Volume Profiles

Focus on specific price zones: Fixed Range Volume Profiles allow traders to concentrate on specific price levels or ranges of particular interest. This targeted approach is especially useful for intraday traders or those who want to analyse short-term price action within particular boundaries.

Adaptability to volatile markets: Time-based Visible Range Volume Profiles may not effectively capture short-term trading activity and liquidity in highly volatile markets. Fixed Range Volume Profiles, on the other hand, can adapt to rapid market movements and provide insights into volume concentrations during significant price fluctuations.

Quick analysis: Since Range Volume Profiles focus on a fixed price range, traders can quickly assess trading activity and volume distribution within that area. It offers a rapid and efficient way to gauge market sentiment and identify critical support and resistance levels.

Benefits of Visible Range Volume Profiles

Natural time-based perspective: Visible Range Volume Profiles are based on periods (e.g., days, weeks or months) and provide a realistic perspective on the market's overall behaviour. This broader view can help traders identify longer-term trends, significant price levels and market structure.

Significant volume areas: Visible Range Volume Profiles highlight areas of the chart with the most substantial trading volume over the specified period. These regions can act as magnets for price and serve as essential reference points for traders.

Consistency across timeframes: Visible Range Volume Profiles maintain consistency across different timeframes. Traders can apply the same principles to analyse volume data regardless of whether they look at daily, weekly or monthly charts.

In summary, the choice between Fixed Range and Visible Range Volume Profiles depends on the trader's trading objectives, time horizon and the level of granularity they seek in their analysis. Both approaches can complement each other and be combined to gain a comprehensive understanding of market dynamics. Whether focusing on short-term price action within specific ranges or studying broader market trends, volume profile analysis can be a powerful tool to enhance trading decisions and market insights.

There are even more volume profile tools.

The image below shows another popular volume profile called Session Volume. It displays a histogram that relates to the volume of the trading session.

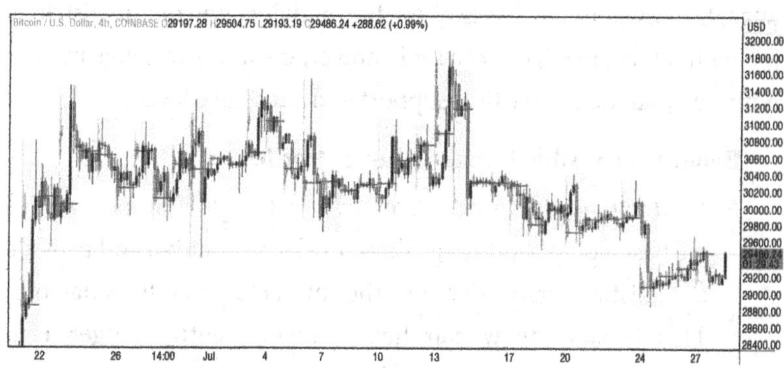

Much like the Fixed Range and the Visible Range, the basic principles are the same, but some advantages of using Session Volume could include the following.

Clear timeframes: Session Volume delineates trading activity within specific timeframes. This clarity benefits intraday traders who want to analyse daily price action and volume dynamics.

Market structure analysis: By focusing on Session Volume, traders can identify critical market structures such as the opening range, closing range and intraday price levels with high liquidity. Understanding these structures can aid in formulating entry and exit points.

Volume-based support and resistance: Session Volume often creates significant support and resistance levels. Traders respect these levels as they indicate intense buying or selling pressure. Incorporating Session Volume can enhance the accuracy of identifying these critical levels.

Confirmation of breakouts and reversals: High-volume breakouts or reversals during a specific session can be more meaningful than extended periods. Session Volume can help confirm the strength of a move, making it more reliable for traders.

Volume profile analysis: Session Volume is integral to volume profile analysis, a technique that visually represents volume at different price levels. Traders can use volume profiles to identify high-volume nodes and areas of price acceptance, aiding in decision-making.

Efficient analysis: Focusing on Session Volume allows traders to analyse the market in smaller, more manageable chunks, leading to more efficient analysis and faster decision-making.

Reduced noise: By concentrating on Session Volume, traders can filter out some of the noise that may be present in longer timeframes. This can lead to more precise insights into short-term market behaviour.

Global market coverage: Different trading sessions correspond to international market openings and closings. Analysing Session

Volume can provide insights into how different regions impact price action during trading hours.

The volume profiles and tools mentioned above are the most popular and the ones many traders could probably already name. Less well-known tools relating to the volume would also include oscillators, for example.

Volume oscillators, such as the Chaikin Money Flow (CMF) or the Volume Rate of Change (VROC), are indicators that combine volume data with price data to generate oscillating values. These indicators help traders identify potential overbought or oversold conditions in the market based on volume patterns. This is just one example of many tools that cross volume and oscillators.

On-Balance Volume (OBV) is another indicator that measures buying and selling pressure. It adds the volume on up days and subtracts it on down days, creating a cumulative line. The idea behind OBV is that changes in the volume trend can precede changes in price direction, providing potential trading signals.

Most wouldn't consider tools such as the Accumulation/Distribution Line (A/D Line) as volume tools, but it does provide another volume technique. The A/D Line evaluates money flow into or out of a security. It considers price and volume to gauge the strength of buying and selling pressure. A rising A/D Line indicates accumulation (buying), while a declining line suggests distribution (selling).

There will be many volume tools I don't cover here. This chapter aims to give you an idea of what volume tools are available rather than lessons on each tool.

In addition to histograms such as fixed range and session, or oscillators like OBV, you also have tools such as the Volume Weighted

Average Price (VWAP). This technical indicator calculates the average price weighted by the trading volume for a given period. Intraday traders often use it to assess the average price a security has traded throughout the day. VWAP can be a reference point for traders to gauge whether a current price is selling above or below the average traded price.

The image below shows the VWAP from the auto-selected level based on the price.

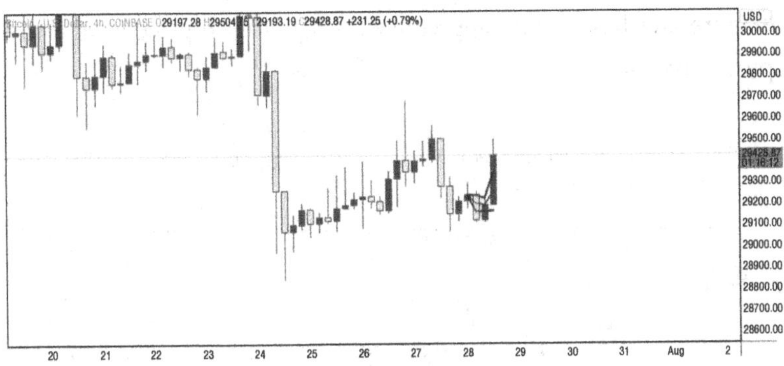

In addition to this, you have the anchored version: Anchored Volume Weighted Average Price (AVWAP).

So, as you can see, there are many tools around volume; most of these are standard and readily available on many charting packages and platforms.

Tools that are less used and only sometimes available on all platforms include Delta, Depth of Market and Footprint.

Delta, or Cumulative Delta, provides a good insight into the overall market sentiment and potential future price movements. In essence, it gives you a view of aggressive buying and selling, and the Delta itself is the net difference between the two.

Aggressive buying occurs when a trader places a market order to buy a financial instrument at the best available price. These orders are executed immediately, taking whatever sell orders are available in the order book.

Aggressive selling happens when a trader places a market order to sell a financial instrument at the best available price, resulting in immediate execution against existing buy orders.

Cumulative Delta is the net difference between the total volume of aggressive buying and aggressive selling at each price level over a specific period.

In the image below, you can see a zero line with the red and green volumes below. This is the most common Cumulative Delta view.

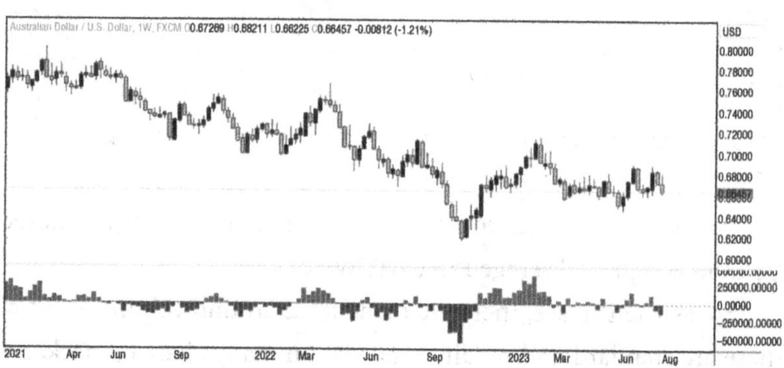

Yet another tool is the Depth of Market (DOM). Also widely known as the Order Book, it is a popular tool to visualise the current market demand and supply for a specific financial instrument. It provides a real-time display of all pending buy and sell orders at different price levels, showing the liquidity available in the market at any given moment.

There is a whole range of software platforms, such as Ninjatrader.com and Sierrachart.com, to name just a couple.

Then there are Footprint charts, which basically combine the regular candlesticks with the volume profile.

Price and volume provide a detailed view of market activity by displaying individual trades at different price levels over a specific period, highlighting the volume traded at each price tick. Footprint charts are vital in analysing order flow and understanding the dynamics between buyers and sellers.

https://optimusfutures.com/tradeblog/archives/footprint-charts
The image below shows an individual candle with the orders inside, next to a regular candlestick whereby you can see the open, high and low, along with the candle close.

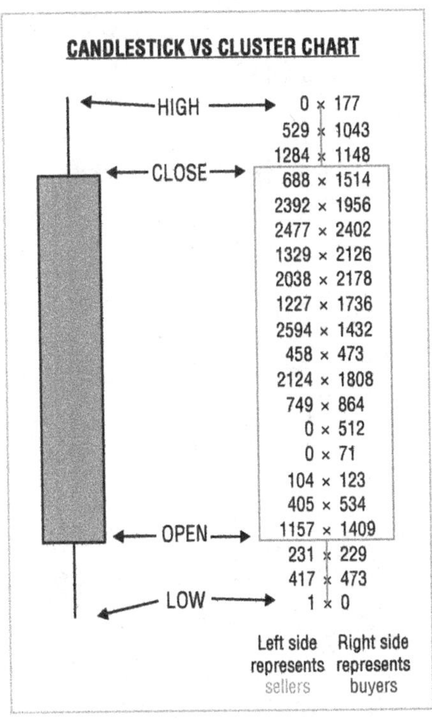

At the end of Chapter 1, I said that the central issue is that people don't know when to use these tools and techniques. What I don't want you to do is jump on your charts and have all of these tools and indicators on the screen. You will get lost, so don't worry if the image above is currently daunting. Knowing they exist is the first step; knowing you can use them is exciting, and learning how to use them is a feeling you don't know yet!

CHAPTER 4

BOTTOM OF THE CHARTS

'Never, ever argue with your trading system.'

—Michael Covel

https://whgzircatlrjxspe.quora.com/Never-ever-argue-with-your-trading-system-Michael-Covel-Meaning-It-will-never-get-you-anywhere-And-let-s-face-it

The X-axis (horizontal axis) typically represents time on the charts. It shows the progression of time from left to right, with each data point or candlestick representing a specific period, such as minutes, hours, days, weeks or months, depending on the chosen timeframe.

I can see you there thinking to yourself; Lewis is stating the obvious here. You're right, I am.

However, time factors play a vital role in some strategies and have no bearing on others. Yet people don't seem to understand how the X-axis can be used to your advantage.

The X-axis shows the historical sequence of price movements over time by progressing from left to right. Traders can analyse market activity during specific periods and identify trends, patterns and historical price levels. Visualise the chart and insert a volume profile as per the previous chapter. This could be a fixed range, visible range or session. The point is to get you thinking about what you see on the chart. Now, step away from that visualisation and think of news events, for example, what happens during a press release, a catastrophic disaster or something as simple as a market slowing down for the holidays.

This isn't easy to visualise, I know. But it's a great exercise to appreciate what we will look for later.

Let me explain.

When the price has been trending for a while, the news is released and the Federal Reserve hikes interest rates. One candle will look out of place with the others on the chart, right? Depending on the timeframe selected, of course.

Now, imagine the chart rallies as we near Friday's close; the number of traders trading that pair will significantly decrease. These events cause things like imbalances, gaps or simple contractions of price. These factors are all part of the game; all too often, the focus is on price. Granted, I often get questions like 'What price, should I go long?' or 'How long should I hold this position?' But rarely is the time factor used in terms of analysis.

As William Delbert Gann once said:

'Time is more important than price. When time is up, price will reverse.'

There are other tools, indicators and strategies created around the time axis. For things like the Fibonacci time zone, there are cycles and combinations of the two, such as the Delta Phenomenon (a sequence based on astrology cycles). https://www.deltasociety.com/content/delta-story

Although it might seem obvious to say, it's not so obvious to think about in the first place—time plays a factor, especially when trading volume. Take the tools covered in the previous chapter; session volume compared to fixed range will yield two very different profiles on your chart.

The reason I felt this topic deserved its own chapter is that it's a topic many forget to take into consideration. Whilst there are cycles that some will give credit to, there are others they may not understand. One of the tools I often use in trading is the COT (Commitment of Traders Report). Knowing what the larger operators are doing is one thing, but knowing a market cycle is another. Imagine a good season for oranges in Florida—lots of significant growth. It had an excellent year; now, stock is abundant during the winter, meaning the price of orange juice throughout the winter 'globally' can stay steady. Flip this on its head. Next year, a terrible hurricane will hit the coast of Florida, and production will be 70% lower than last year. What will this do for the prices come winter?

Another thing to keep in mind in terms of the time axis is, of course, standard business hours. From Asia opening whilst the United States was still asleep to European offices opening a few hours later,

London traders started an hour later. Then, they went to New York while the Europeans were on lunch.

These things can affect your trading, depending on your timeframe, hold time, etc. If you trade Forex, there are spread hours—essentially, this is the end-of-day settlement. I am sure many brokers use this to hunt stops. But knowing it's there will stop you from getting caught out.

As you will see in later chapters, allotting time for the volume will increase your overall understanding of what is happening on the chart and why. Seeing the delta from one candle to another is like seeing a magic trick for the first time. As you get to appreciate the logic more and more, each subcategory I have as chapters in this book will make a little more sense. I've had people tell me this is like peeking into the Matrix. To be fair, it almost is.

To conclude this chapter, I will say don't underestimate the X-axis's power, but don't ever think you can master it. You must strike a balance and know what time factors affect the market you are trading, from spread hours to cycles and most things in between.

So often, people come to me at the end of a stream or direct message me and ask for guidance on things like 'When will distribution be done then?' or 'How long do you think this accumulation will take?' Whilst the time factor is essential, it's less critical on a bigger scale. Of course, spread hours, news events and other blips on the chart can be triggered, but they are not all that noticeable when you zoom out. Logic is all you need; if accumulation is done in 5 minutes, do you think the price can rally and rally and keep rallying? It's like only putting £5 of fuel in your car and expecting to drive thousands of miles.

I thought this was important to cover in the book because when talking about volume profiles, time can be a factor; not just the amount of time but, for example, how many candles you have on the chart will affect a volume profile such as visible range. Another example could be using profiles that go too far back, which might affect the 'real' sensitivity of the data you're viewing live.

CHAPTER 5

MARKET MAKERS

'Don't worry about what the markets are going to do; worry about what you are going to do in response to the markets.'

—Michael Carr

https://hugosway.com/dont-worry-about-what-the-markets-are-going-to-do-worry-about-what-you-are-going-to-do-in-response-to-the-markets-michael-carr-2

Market makers are financial entities, often brokerage firms or specialised trading firms, that facilitate the buying and selling of instruments in the stock market. They ensure liquidity and smooth trading operations in the market. Or at least this is the market definition. Market makers are responsible for maintaining a continuous bid and asking the price for a specific set of securities, allowing investors to execute trades quickly and efficiently.

Here are some aspects of market makers and their role in the stock market:

Liquidity Provision. Market makers act as intermediaries between buyers and sellers. They continuously quote, bid and ask prices for particular securities, indicating the prices they are willing to buy or sell. This constant availability of buy and sell orders helps ensure a secure market, making it easier for investors to buy or sell shares at any time.

Bid-Ask Spread. Market makers make money through the bid-ask spread, which is the difference between the price they are willing to buy (the bid) and the price they are ready to sell (the ask). Market makers profit from this spread by providing liquidity and taking on the risk of holding an inventory of securities.

Order Execution. When a trader places an order to buy or sell a security, the market maker matches the order with an opposite order in their inventory or seeks another market participant with a matching order. This process ensures the trade is executed promptly, contributing to market efficiency.

Price Stability. Market makers help maintain price stability by absorbing imbalances in supply and demand. Market makers step in to provide liquidity and prevent large price swings during increased volatility or low liquidity periods.

NYSE Specialists. On the New York Stock Exchange (NYSE), specialists play a similar role to market makers. They are exchange members responsible for facilitating trading in specific listed stocks and maintaining an orderly market. There are three excellent books by author Richard Ney asserting that market makers manipulate the market to the detriment of the average investor: (1) *The Wall Street Jungle*; (2) *The Wall Street Gang*; (3) *Making It in the Market*.

Other markets also have market makers or specialists:

NASDAQ Market Makers. In the NASDAQ stock market, market makers are individuals or firms that provide liquidity for specific stocks. They are responsible for updating and maintaining bid and ask quotes and are integral to NASDAQ's electronic trading system.

It's important to note that while market makers enhance market liquidity and efficiency, they are not immune to conflicts of interest. Sometimes, market makers may act in their self-interest, mainly if they are dealing with proprietary trading strategies or market-making algorithms. However, regulations and oversight aim to ensure fair and transparent practices in the market.

Although it is not quite the same, other entities can manipulate markets. Brokers and exchanges, for example. As I mentioned in the previous chapter about spread hours. You will sometimes see these scams wick up or down on an instrument; they might stop you (out) and reverse in the other direction.

Going back to the books by Richard Ney, it's a similar concept to Elliott Wave Theory or Wyckoff techniques. Although markets are made up of sentiment, the question needs to be asked: Who's controlling the narrative? Fake news, FED hikes, inflation and so on. Wyckoff used the term Composite Man.

What Wyckoff meant by this is institutional traders or large market players who move the markets. Hence, market makers.

According to Wyckoff's theory, the Composite Man represents the collective actions of major players such as institutional investors, banks and other large financial entities. He believed that the Composite Man leaves behind footprints in the price and volume data, which can be observed and analysed to gain insight into the market's future direction.

For me, this is a huge factor. As the saying goes, 'the trend is your friend'. Understanding more about the market makers will help you pick that trend direction.

In 2021, I wrote several articles publicly available on TradingView highlighting the presence of institutional money flowing into Bitcoin. This is relevant here because by knowing what the more prominent players were aiming to do, you could anticipate the next moves. The first article talked about re-accumulation: https://www.tradingview.com/chart/idea/P0t1Wz75/

The image shows where the immutable post was made, talking about the re-accumulation happening at the time.

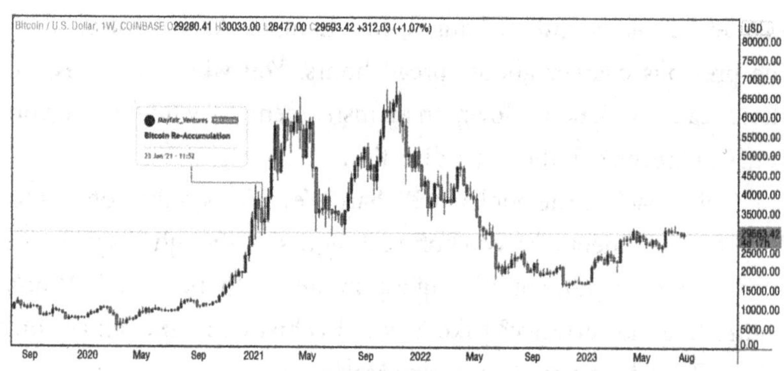

Understanding—even acknowledging—that the market makers were present meant I could give a direction in which the market would likely move next.

In the next article, I explained why the price would drop from the region we were in. This came down to knowing a specific Wyckoff schematic was forming. As you can see, I named this post 'They blew up the rocket'. Calls for the moon were all over social media at the time.

The image shows the following article on TradingView explaining the reason behind an imminent drop.

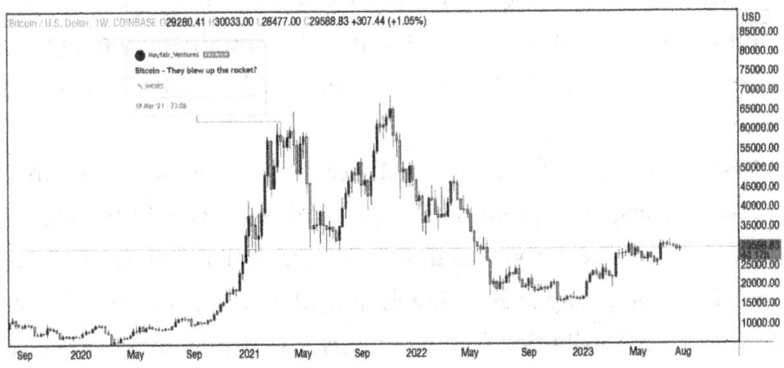

https://www.tradingview.com/chart/idea/GWjR3Sam/

The reason I have shared these here is not to say, 'Hey, look at me, I did a thing', but to emphasise the importance of knowing the reasons behind these types of moves.

I often see posts from influencers on social media with claims like 'Bitcoin will be $100k by the end of the year'. One, they have no logic to back up the price expectation, and two, why would the end of the year be a factor? What you need to understand about market makers is that these guys can stay in a market an awful lot longer than the retail trader, trading from his bedroom.

Compared to the stock market, crypto is another world. Crypto has other factors working behind the scenes, such as the fact that there is an 'on-chain' matrix term in the context of finance or blockchain technology. This is a specific concept or metric related to blockchain data analysis; it is challenging to provide a particular explanation. Other than 'on-chain', it typically refers to data or transactions that occur directly on the blockchain, as opposed to 'off-chain' transactions outside the blockchain network.

Algorithms and tools have been designed to spoof the data, adding large buys or sells to attract the price and then removing the orders. This is basically a more advanced market maker in another form.

Back to Wyckoff, and you will see how the logic can fit into market makers, more prominent players and spoof-type technologies.

First of all, the market needs time for accumulation and distribution. The Composite Man is involved in the market's accumulation (buying) and distribution (selling) phases. These phases occur before a significant trend reversal or a major move in the market.

Second, Wyckoff emphasised the importance of analysing price and volume data to understand the intentions of the Composite Man. Sudden changes in volume or price action may indicate the Composite Man's activities, as my TradingView articles showed.

Third, Wyckoff identified different market phases, such as accumulation, markup (uptrend), distribution and markdown (downtrend). By understanding these phases, traders can align their strategies with the prevailing market sentiment. At the start and end of these phases, the market returns to accumulation or distribution (depending on the direction and where the Composite Man wants the price to go next). These phases are called Wyckoff Schematics.

Wyckoff developed his visual representations to illustrate the typical price and volume patterns associated with accumulation and distribution phases. I covered the schematics in detail in *Master the Art of Trading*. All you need to know here is that they exist, and the reason they exist is to help the market makers/Composite Man buy the stock they want or sell the stock they already have for profit.

As I said earlier, I want this to be a chatty type of read. You will bring these components together as you advance in the book. At the end of this chapter, I want you to visualise how the market makers can control a chart in terms of both price candles and volume. Please give it some thought before you start the next chapter.

CHAPTER 6

END OF NEW YORK BUSINESS DAYS

'Amateurs think about how much money they can make. Professionals think about how much money they could lose.'

—Jack Schwager

https://hugosway.com/amateurs-think-about-how-much-money-they-can-make-professionals-think-about-how-much-money-they-could-lose-jack-schwager

As I mentioned about the time factor in Chapter 4, another critical aspect of trading is knowing when liquidity will likely come to the market.

In essence, the end of trading days in New York is a critical juncture where traders, investors and analysts assess the day's developments, make decisions based on closing prices and prepare for the next trading session. It's a time when market participants react to the news, adjust their positions and set the stage for the market's behaviour in the following days.

New York has more of an impact than other regions due to its location, technically being the last to close after Asia, Europe and London.

In addition, it is also well aligned with other major financial centres, such as London and Frankfurt. This alignment allows smoother transitions between trading sessions and creates periods of overlap with higher activity levels. We are emphasising the time leading up to the close in New York, preparing for tomorrow's opening as such.

Other essential factors could include the *level of media coverage* in the United States; due to its significance in the financial world, events and developments during the New York trading session tend to receive extensive media coverage. This media attention can amplify the impact of news and events on market sentiment.

Increased volatility: the period leading up to the close of the New York trading session tends to experience increased trading activity and volatility. This can be attributed to traders making last-minute decisions, adjusting their positions and reacting to news or events throughout the trading day—again, think of the impact whilst the markets are closed and what Asia will wake up to in a few hours.

This is the time in markets such as forex where you have what is known as 'price reconciliation'. The closing price of a security or currency pair is crucial for many purposes, including calculating daily returns, assessing portfolio performance and executing various trading strategies. Traders and investors often analyse the closing price to gauge market sentiment and decide their positions for the following trading day.

End-of-day orders: many traders place orders to buy or sell securities or currencies at the closing price. These orders can impact the market, potentially causing price fluctuations as they are executed.

Just like the price reconciliation, you also then have overnight developments. Specifically for the forex market, the end of the New York trading session marks the start of an overnight period when other financial markets worldwide are active. Economic data releases, geopolitical events and news can occur during this time, affecting currency prices when the markets reopen.

Gap analysis: traders often look for gaps between the closing price of one trading day and the opening price of the next. These gaps can provide valuable information about market sentiment and potential price direction.

In summary, you have several reasons why New York sessions and the end of business in New York are key. Knowing this and assessing your trade setups can save you from wild spreads as markets reconcile.

Trading during the London/New York cross-over is a good time if you're in Europe or Eastern America, as you have a much higher volume on average to take advantage of.

Although the London session seems to have a lot of volume, you may see a trend reverse or strengthen during UK business hours. The key, for me, is New York.

Why didn't I add this to the X-axis chapter?! It's different, and I wanted you to see them as separate. What I said in Chapter 5 about how market makers can make price candles or volume profiles look. It's all about liquidity, although big moves don't happen on small timeframes. You can bet that it will be during peak liquidity when they do. There are people with full-blown strategies around trading these sessions or executing a trade only during these sessions.

The takeaway is that in previous chapters, you have built up a visual aid that brings together the various types of volume profiles, what the X-axis is, market makers and high liquidity times. Can you see why timing and how you deploy a fixed range volume tool can be used to your advantage? Trust me, it's coming!

CHAPTER 7

HOW TO SPOT VOLUME WITHOUT INDICATORS

This isn't magic; it's actually easier than you think. Of course, there is an advantage to having the volume displayed on the charts, but when you know how to spot it without any tools, the charts seem to open up a whole new world of possibilities.

To understand this, you first need to understand the dynamics that move the market; this, in turn, will help you see the various types of volume.

As I explained in Chapter 5, the market makers play games with retail traders but, in doing so, leave behind an obvious footprint.

In the next chapter, I will cover the technical side of this (which is known as Wyckoff) but first, let's look at how different momentum affects what gets printed on the chart itself.

Without using illustrations (I believe this to be a more powerful way for you to comprehend this), first visualise each candle like a football field (soccer, if that's your thing). Now imagine territory controlled and time spent in each half. If you now flip this visualisation into a 2D view in your head, you have the green team on the lower half and the red team on the top half.

As the game (candlestick) plays out, you know the time factor involved. If you're viewing a daily timeframe, your candle represents a day; if you're looking at 4-hour candles, then your game is 4 hours.

Now imagine the game being played. As the price rises, the green team is pushing into the red team's territory. If the match finishes there, the red team lose and the candle closes green.

Now imagine the same scenario, but the pitch can be extended. The further one team goes, the more momentum the game gains and the more the candle extends. I hope you can see why I said it's best to visualise this in your head. It's a simple analogy and effective in helping you understand the dynamics of the movement. Think of it like the green team below and the red team on top, much like a sports game playing left to right.

If this makes sense to you, it will be so much easier to understand how volume now plays. Although not always true, the more the volume, the larger the extension. Meaning the more significant the candle becomes.

That said, if you see one of two anomalies in the volume, this is also a great indication. What I mean by this is if you are watching a chart and the volume is large, but the candle remains small, what is going on? Why is there no extension? Indeed, high volume equals larger candles. In simple terms, buyers and sellers agree on a price with a small range. I like to call these 'auction areas'.

The opposite of this is minimal volume and massive price movements one way or the other. What does this mean? Well, if we use an example of, let's say, 100. Suppose the price rallies to 105. Buyers are interested and demand is being met, but buyers are happy to buy again at 105 and, say, 108. In that case, the price carries through to 110, so whilst the demand is filled with the supply available, it means the sellers are not yet actively selling and are trying to push the price lower. Essentially, they are happy to sell the anomalies to buyers at higher prices, and buyers seem just as excited to buy at higher prices.

In my first scenario, the price narrows and what tends to happen is maybe this goes on for a handful of candles, in essence making a tightish range. This range (the auction area) is likely to be a level of interest in the future. The logic for this is simple: both buyers and sellers were interested at these prices.

Imagine the price runs up from this high-volume zone; it rallies two or three candles. This would suggest the buyers are in control, and the zone was an area of overall accumulation. However, there will be shorts that were opened there and stops from the buys just below these levels. After a rally, where could you imagine the price will want to head?

In the example below, I will show you some clusters that create an auction area, and then I will add a fixed range volume profile showing the move away and back to the zones.

As you can see in this image, there is a move from the zone highlighted with a box and back to the zone.

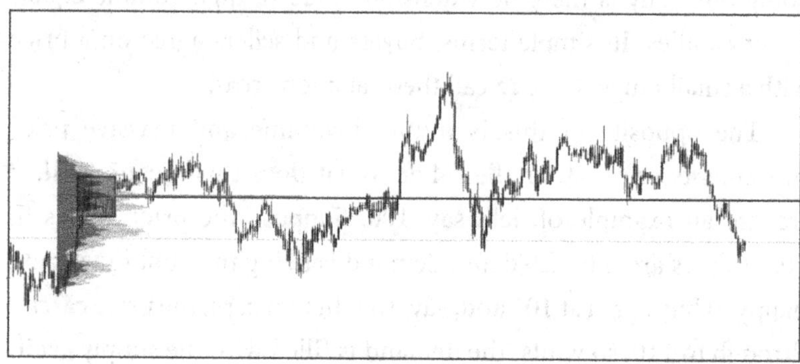

So, by explaining the two scenarios, you can now see how auction areas pull back prices. It becomes much more apparent where volume 'happened'. Now what you need to do as an exercise is take a naked chart and draw rectangles from these areas. For example, you could use one colour for the high-volume cluster with low-price nodes and another for the price going fast in one direction. This is known as an imbalance. First, take a higher timeframe chart, let's say a daily. And from a swing high or low, you want to backtest this on the current move. See the example below.

This image draws the volume profile tool from the swing high down to the low. Price continues up, seeking high-volume nodes.

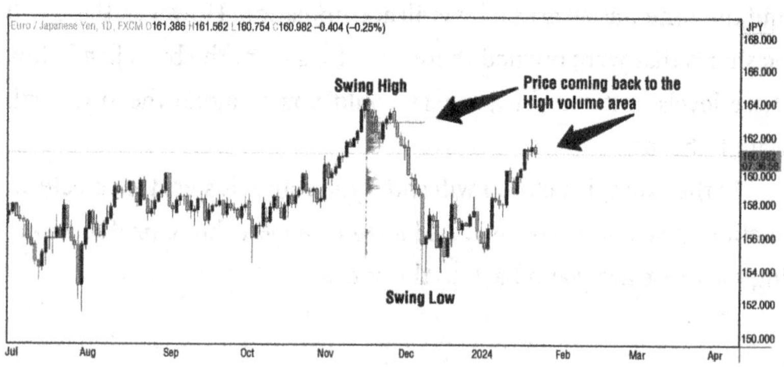

Once the prior swing is marked out, what backtest happens as you play it forward?

It will take a little time to train your eyes, but trust me, you will ultimately see the charts differently than you currently do.

Although there is not much benefit from not using the volume indicators, this exercise will help you understand how to use these indicators better, as now you know what you're looking for.

Many trading books or educational videos give you the how, not the why. When you understand this, it is now a matter of using it to your advantage. If you can identify these critical levels by eye before you set off to do your complete analysis, you have the essential levels mapped out. This can help you determine if we are likely seeing a distribution or an accumulation. This level of analysis can be done on any chart, in any timeframe and can be scanned in seconds.

When you read the following two chapters, this will make even more sense! If you are unsure what you are looking for, I strongly advise you to go back to the start of this chapter and reread it before jumping to Wyckoff and master patterns.

CHAPTER 8

WYCKOFF

'Every artist was first an amateur.'

—Ralph Waldo Emerson

https://fineartviews.com/blog/149161/every-artist-was-first-an-amateur

In the early twentieth century Richard D. Wyckoff, a stock market trader and educator, developed a market blueprint reflecting what drives a stock's price movement. The Wyckoff method is based on the idea that the price and volume movements in the market are not random but driven by the activities of large institutional players and intelligent money. Remember what you read about market makers?

In simple terms, you will notice times when the price is either up, down or sideways. A lot of the time the market is sideways, and people need help understanding this. What we are witnessing is either some accumulation or distribution.

Wyckoff believed that market prices move through cycles of accumulation (smart money buying) and distribution (smart money selling). These phases are critical in determining the future direction of an asset. Then, naturally, you would expect a markup or a markdown.

Richard Wyckoff developed a series of charts and patterns depicting the accumulation and distribution stages. These include the Accumulation and Distribution Schematic, which traders use to identify potential entry and exit points. It's what happens and how it happens that makes all the difference.

In *Master the Art of Trading*, I covered the basics of Wyckoff terminology and how to view it from the fundamental level. But let's go on and explain in detail what makes it work and why.

This image shows simple Wyckoff logic.

https://medium.com/algorithmic-trading/how-stock-price-trends-are-driven-primarily-by-institutional-operators-who-manipulate-stock-prices-d3795b2116da

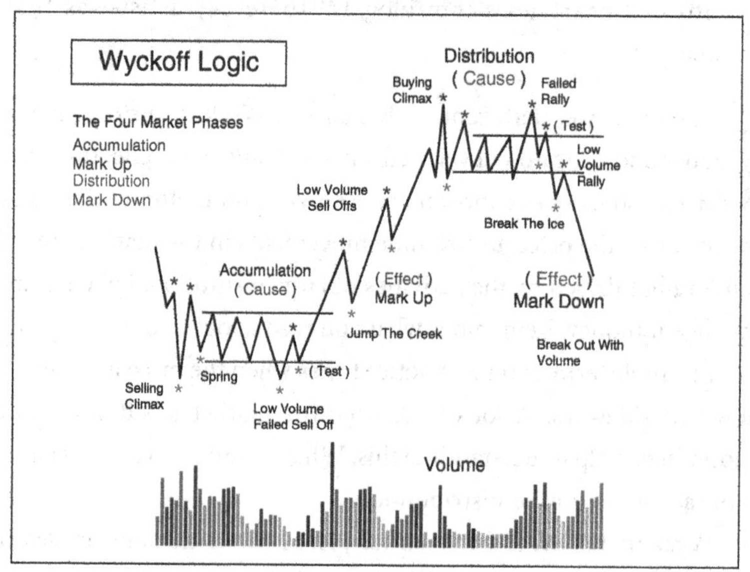

First, there are typically four phases within the Wyckoff method.

Accumulation Phase. This is when smart money accumulates a position, often at lower prices. During this phase, the price tends to trade in a range or consolidate.

Markup Phase. After accumulation, there is an uptrend as smart money begins to push prices higher.

Distribution Phase. In this phase, smart money starts selling its positions to the public. Prices often trade in a range or show signs of distribution.

Markdown Phase. Following distribution, there's a downtrend as prices fall.

One of the things I teach inside Discord and in my first book is how you can combine Elliott Waves to give hints as to the likelihood of an accumulation over a distribution. Spotting whether you are in a distribution or an accumulation phase is likely the most challenging part for everyone when using the Wyckoff method.

The primary issue for many traders when looking into Wyckoff techniques is the inability to spot which phase you are in. The schematics seem obvious after completion, but when they are complete it's sometimes too late. Although Wyckoff himself traded the exit of the pattern, there are opportunities within the schematic in which a trader can profit.

Volume analysis is also central to the Wyckoff method. Analysing volume patterns can provide insights into the strength or weakness of a price move. This, of course, will help spot the buying or the selling, but again there's a lot more to it!

All too often I have seen new traders come to me or talk about Wyckoff on platforms such as Twitter. They think they have mastered something after spotting a likely schematic—only for them to be wrong in terms of the location or type of the schematic.

In March 2021, I called a Wyckoff Distribution Schematic for Bitcoin. My social media comments were all negative; I was anti-Bitcoin and all that! Many other analysts called the move around $60,000 a re-accumulation. Unfortunately for them, they had missed one obvious candle, one obvious tell-tale sign as to the distribution schematic being in play and not the accumulation one.

It helped that I had already seen the re-accumulation move and called it much earlier.

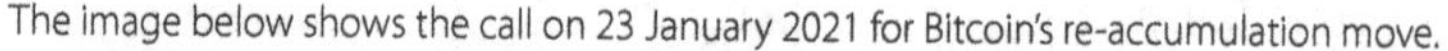
The image below shows the call on 23 January 2021 for Bitcoin's re-accumulation move.

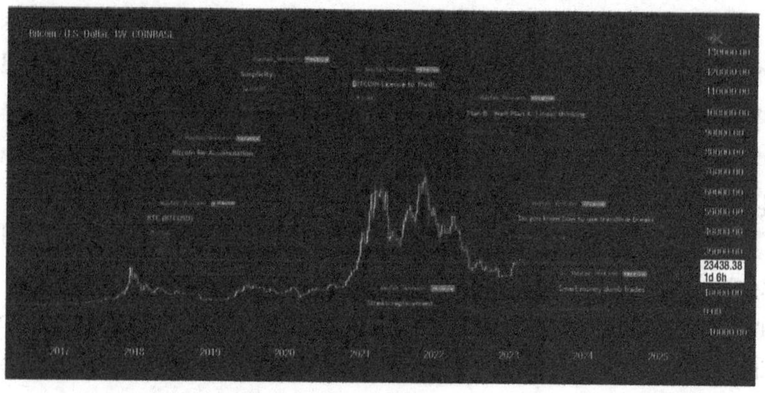

The next move becomes more apparent. I want you to visualise the thinking behind the swings again. Let me walk you through this.

Step 1. Let's assume an uptrend. In one of his books, Richard Ney used a great example of a warehouse owner buying wholesale and selling to retail for this scenario. In Step 1 the larger operators want to buy stock without letting everyone know they are buying. This, of course, is an accumulation. (I'll cover the schematics after this visualisation process.)

Step 2. We saw an accumulation, and a markup followed it. A Bull run.

Step 3. Composite Man will want to take some profits here and ensure retail doesn't know where next. We have extended a good amount from the accumulation and started going sideways. This, of course, is the re-accumulation. The price rallies for a smaller markup. Bringing us to Step 5. . . . Yes, I missed Step 4 as that was the markup, and most retailers miss it!

Step 5. We are now into the first significant distribution; profits are taken from the initial accumulation and re-accumulation. Composite Man's only issue is that selling too much too soon will drop the price too fast. He needs to remain in control. So, the price will fall fast and reject rather violently back up and then slowly back into the re-distribution area, giving us Step 6 (markdown) and Step 7 (re-distribution).

Inside the re-distribution, retail traders will be thinking to themselves 'the price is yet to make a lower low, we still have a high from the top, the market looks and feels bullish, and this was only a pullback'.

We go sideways for a while, even moving up slightly with an ascending pattern. Then, for Step 8, the following markdown is done.

Now, I could make this very visual and have diagrams and charts, but I choose not to because if you can picture this happening, it will make more sense to you. Seeing it on the chart, your mind will glance at it, assume you know it and move on to the next bit. By using this visualisation technique, I hope to get the picture over to you, supported by logic. In these eight simple steps, you can understand exactly why.

If you want to see the picture, here you go.

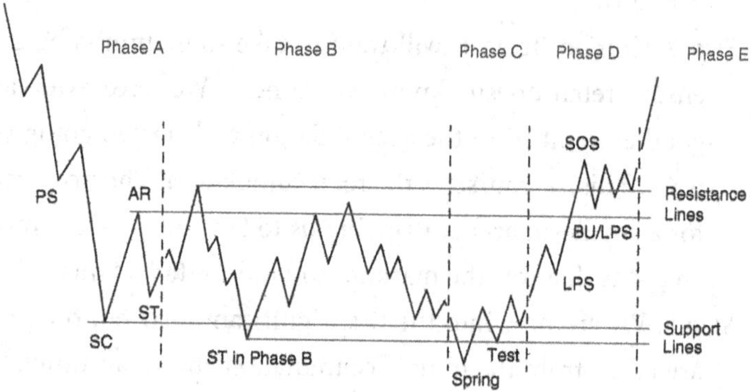

The Wyckoff method is considered a holistic approach to trading and investing because it combines price, volume and market sentiment analysis. It aims to help traders and investors make more informed decisions by understanding the market's underlying dynamics. However, like all trading methods, it has its strengths and limitations, and success with the Wyckoff method requires practice, experience and ongoing refinement of your skills.

So please don't just skip this. Don't look at the schematics and assume you know it. When I teach this in person, it's all too easy to want to apply it to the charts.

You have a good starting point once you can identify the accumulation versus the distribution. This can be done using techniques such as Elliott Wave Theory and knowing where we will likely move up or down. It can also be volume analysis and understanding if we see more buying or selling during the range-bound periods.

In this image, you can see where we would expect to see distribution and accumulation based on the EW theory.

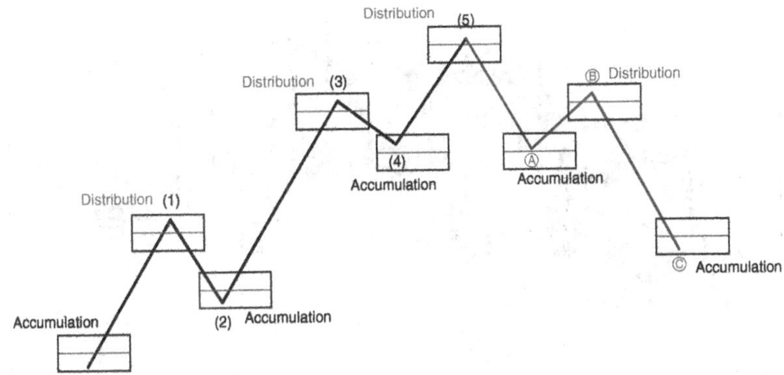

Inside a schematic, you will see a pattern form that can be mirrored. If it's coming from below, we have likely seen an accumulation. Spot the re-accumulation and wait for the distribution signs. In an example of a distribution, you are likely to see a strong rejection after a healthy rally. This is the Automatic Reaction (AR) from the Buyer's Climax (BC). When it's an accumulation, this is known as the Automatic Rally, but both are marked (AR). The general gist is that it's the first sign of character change. You would assume it's a heavy, knee-jerk reaction to a price target Composite Man (CM). Retail, of course, is buying every drop and CM profit-taking—selling to the retail traders there with open arms and wallets.

As the price moves down, retail traders will say things like 'buy the dip; it's only a pullback'.

Earlier, I mentioned calling the drop from $65,000 down in Bitcoin. In the image below, you can see the AR move shown here by the downward-facing arrow on the left, followed by several red candles.

Distribution schematic in play (Bitcoin, March 2021).

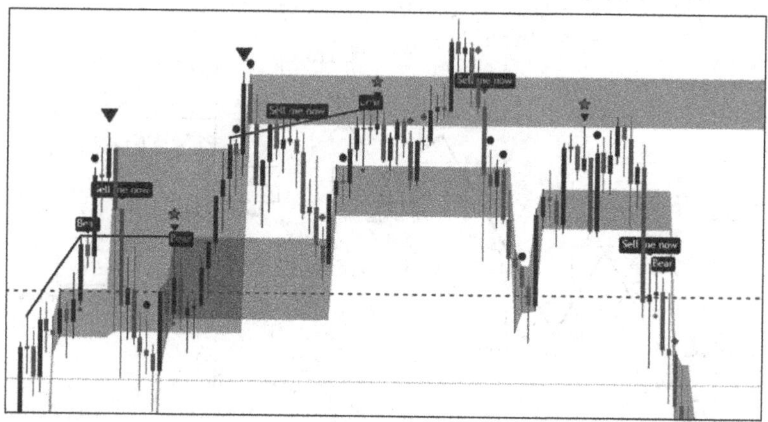

The move down showed the force, which wasn't likely just a distribution pullback. Again, we had already seen the re-accumulation give an outstanding clue as to the start of the distribution phase, which was NOW.

What you see next is designed to make you, as a retail trader, think we are about to continue up. In other words, the next move tends to provide false hope.

Again, I want you to think long and hard about this aspect. What would give false hope to a retail trader here? Well, a new high, of course. For many, the new high is higher, and the uptrend is likely to continue. But for us in the know, we have reached a level whereby distribution is to be expected; we have seen the BC and the AR. The high is simply run-on liquidity designed to attract new active buyers. But, in Wyckoff's terms, the move from the AR is to make it look like an A, B and C move, as expected in other disciplines such as Elliott Wave Theory. Retail traders will use Fibonacci retracement levels, see the .618 move and flip it to an extension. Nine times out of ten, these fib levels of extensions and retracements will be precisely where you would expect. Now the reversal comes, and we shoot off to make the new high. Buyers who bought the dip A, B and C move now think it's their lucky day! Prices make new highs, attracting even more buyers. . . This was the set of retail traders who were too scared to get in on the low. Instead, they waited for confirmation. This triggers a new reaction. In Wyckoff's terms, it's known as the Up Thrust (UT).

A UT occurs when the price of an asset briefly moves above a critical resistance level or a significant trading range and then quickly reverses and closes below that level. Essentially, it's a false breakout to the upside.

Characteristics of an Upthrust. (1) It often occurs in high volume, a sign of selling pressure. (2) It traps bullish traders who see the breakout and buy into the market, only to be caught off guard when the price quickly reverses. (3) The close of the candle or bar is below the resistance level, indicating that the breakout was not sustained.

Keep all of this in mind. . . .

Now, at this stage in the schematic, you can build a solid foundation for what you expect to see next. Wyckoff just watched this part and waited a little longer for the price—to confirm we were following. But as you have already spotted the distribution, the BC, and hopefully are watching the AR in real time, here's where risk versus reward is a factor. You could target a short entry with a kind of tight stop loss, or you can do as Wyckoff himself did and wait for more confirmation. Of course, you can have an image or PDF next to you; I occasionally put a semi-transparent image of the chart next to the price. So don't stress about trying to remember all of this.

The price will likely come down a little here and head back towards the lower half of the schematic, meaning you could take a narrow, short position. But as the price shows weakness, the schematic is not complete. Not enough liquidity is available for a drop with any real intent. Instead, the price will drop to the lower bands and likely rise again, adding to the false belief.

Bitcoin is a prime example—everyone wants it to go up and keep going up. So, when they see a higher low from the UT, compared to the AR move, it's another sign of 'for retail' and the dip should be bought! As before, we move up again and create another higher high. Why does this happen? For the same reason as before, it moves up to sucker new positions both from the sign of weakness low and, of course, new entries sat at the UT highs. Within the schematic, if you zoom into a timeframe (assume you are watching these moves daily), take a step down to the 4-hour chart. These moves up will be disguised as impulsive moves. You have to think like a professional trader here. Most retail thinks like retail and will see these moves in smaller timeframes. For most, it's all about the action now.

As we rally to a new high, this is the Up Thrust After Distribution (UTAD), often accompanied by increased trading volume, particularly when the price moves above the resistance level. The surge in volume reflects the participation of traders who believed in the breakout and bought into the market. This is the fuel for the drop.

Of course, you will have the buyers every time the price slows down within the schematic on its way out. But this is now a lost cause for the buyers. Expect the price to go down and create what's known as the Last Points of Supply (LPSY) before exiting the schematic support boundaries.

When I first wrote *Master the Art of Trading*, I wanted a simple chronological breakdown for traders of any level to feel comfortable using Wyckoff. I was reluctant to go into the 'why', but hope the logic comes flooding through as you read this chapter.

The whole market is a sequence. Some will say it's an algorithm seeking liquidity; these levels of liquidity can be spotted and used to your advantage. Once you can identify the likelihood of a distribution or an accumulation, the liquidity on smaller timeframes becomes apparent. As mentioned earlier, I personally like combining the Elliott Wave Principles with the Wyckoff methodology.

Use the Elliott Wave Theory to give you a higher probability of the type of schematic you are likely to see form. Say, 'I expect accumulation and not distribution here, as we are at low 2 or 4 regions in Elliott terms'.

Here's how obvious it was in that Bitcoin call from March 2021 I mentioned above.

March 2021: Bitcoin is calling the drop. Mayfair Ventures on TradingView: 'They blew up the rocket'.

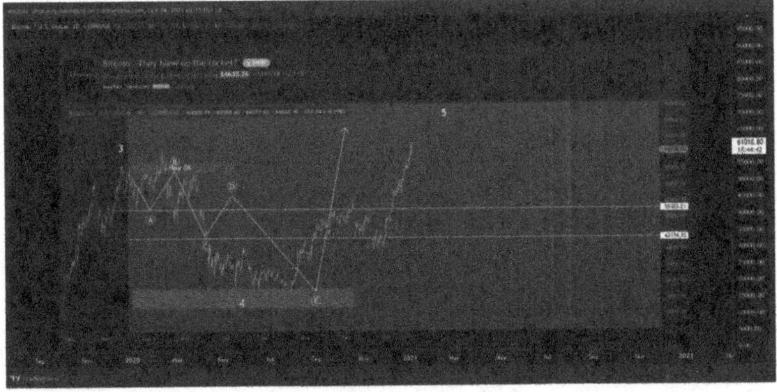

Not only was the impending drop noticeable to spot, but the levels of liquidity were also. As marked (4) and (E) in the image above, the market sought its liquidity level before going back up.

You will notice from the image that to the left of the 3 we saw the BC; the 3 itself was the UT and to the right of the 3 you had the UTAD. So, whilst it might not be evident at first, when you know we are looking at these levels for a plausible distribution, the Elliott Wave Theory highlights this area.

CHAPTER 9

MASTER PATTERNS

'The game of speculation is the most uniformly fascinating in the world. But it is not a game for the stupid, the mentally lazy, the person of inferior emotional balance, or the get-rich-quick adventurer. They will die poor.'

—Jesse Livermore

https://quotefancy.com/quote/1639486/Jesse-Lauriston-Livermore-The-game-of-speculation-is-the-most-uniformly-fascinating-game

There is another way of seeing these Wyckoff schematics, that is, as a master pattern. This is like a dumbed-down Wyckoff schematic, in essence. It's based on the Wyckoff methodology. Without being exposed to all the technical aspects of Wyckoff's methodology, you can see the narrowing of the price into a range that creates a master pattern. In other words, it's Wyckoff without calling it

Wyckoff or trying to identify each swing within the schematic. This is precisely why I like to call it a dumbed-down Wyckoff view. This can be viewed again on any timeframe, on any chart or instrument.

I will show an example, but before I do, think about this: the price is increasing. Let's assume we are watching a 4-hour chart as the price increases, one green candle, then a second green candle. You notice the third is a little smaller than the first two. The next candle might be red and at a similar level to the top and bottom of the green candle before it. If you zoom in a little, say a 30-minute chart, you will see the two candles on the 4 hours are making highs and lows and lows and highs within that region (obvious, right?). So if you draw a box around the zone or range, mark the 50% level of this range. Mark it out and extend it to the right. What you have is a contraction of price, so although spotted on the 4 hours, we have eight candles in that range on the 30-minute chart. We had a green and a red candle of similar size on the 4-hour chart.

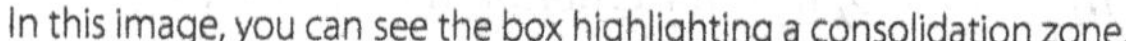
In this image, you can see the box highlighting a consolidation zone.

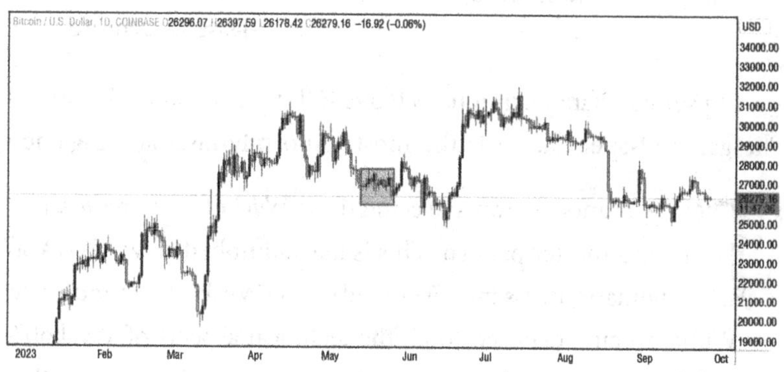

The price on the higher timeframe will look like a handful of bars compared to several here, as shown.

As I mentioned above, I then extended the 50% level of the box over to the right, just like the image below.

This image shows the box along with the 50% level marked out.

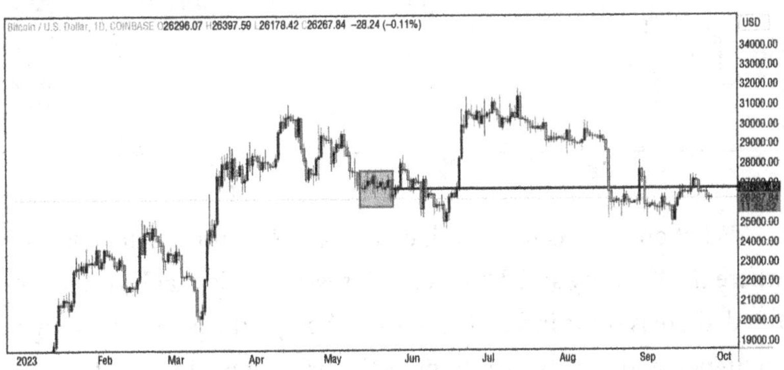

You will find that moving away from your box will have price travel roughly equidistant down and up or up and down. This is known as the expansion phase. In essence, you are witnessing a schematic on a more minor degree, seen on the higher timeframe chart. As the price tightens, it is seeking liquidity. In the example image I used here, the price goes up and attracts longs; it creates a new low, taking stops and triggering new shorts—all of which before moving up rapidly above the old highs on the left. Again, ask yourself, what is happening here and why?

The answer is, it's now grabbing more considerable liquidity to the upside after moving from the downside—this repeats repeatedly.

The image on the next page shows how the price is pulled back to the 50% level.

I show how the price from the top is pulled back to the equilibrium line.

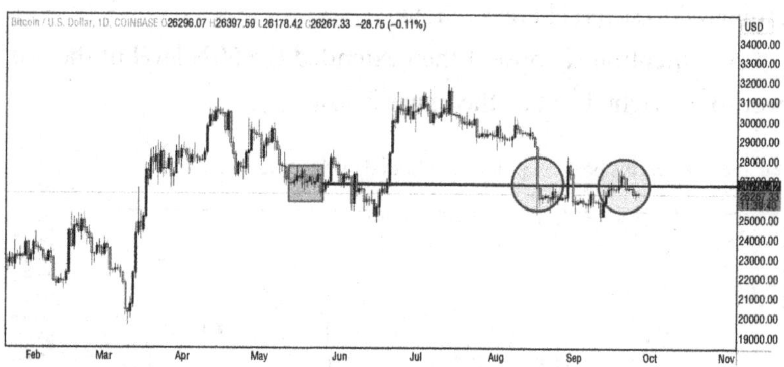

What does it mean? Why does it happen? Again, it's all to do with where the liquidity sits. Think of it this way: inside that box we identified, there is some indecision; buyers thought the price was going to go higher, and sellers tried to push the price down lower. There will be trapped traders for each move, and new orders will be set in this position.

Here is the raw form of the master pattern.

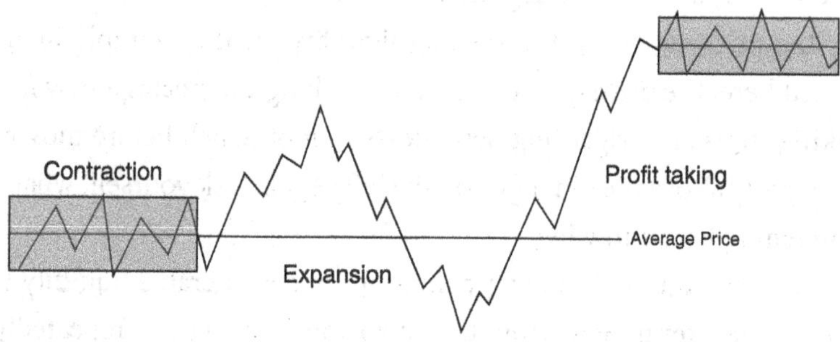

I hope you now see how some of these things can fit together. The general idea is not to overcomplicate trading; it's often better when you think 'less is more'. Fewer indicators, less time on the charts and better trades.

You have learned in this book already that you can identify distribution or accumulation. You know the logic as to why Composite Man acts the way he does and how it's similar to Richard Ney's example of filling the warehouse or selling the stock in that warehouse to retail. You can even spot levels without the use of an indicator. Knowing what happens inside a Wyckoff schematic will allow you to see them as master patterns instead of something more complex.

All I need you to realise is that the market is an algorithm seeking liquidity. Once you get your head around that. You are indeed on your way.

If you follow my streams or have read my TradingView posts, I often talk about 'auction areas'. These, for me, could be Wyckoff, distribution areas, supply or demand levels, master patterns or accumulation areas. They are much the same. They equal an area where people take pride in both buying and selling. Both parties have some interest at these levels. Regardless of terminology, the concepts and rules remain the same. The market needs to grab liquidity from below before it can travel up and show intent to the upside before it's likely to fall. Think back to Chapter 5 on market makers, or what a Wyckoff spring or UTAD does to retail. Can you see how these things start to come together?

CHAPTER 10

VOLUME SHAPES

'The main purpose of the stock market is to make fools of as many men as possible.'

—Bernard Baruch

https://www.brainyquote.com/quotes/bernard_baruch_181388

This image shows volume profile.

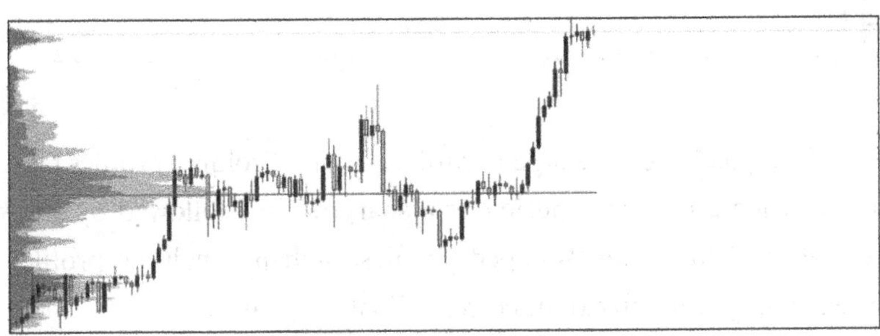

You might have seen volume profiles on a chart; you might even have used volume profiles on your charts. But do you know how to read them? Do you know that various signs in the profile can be used to your advantage?

Let's take a look at some of the shapes.

P-shaped volume profiles often manifest when a market experiences a rapid ascent followed by a consolidation phase. As the price reaches the upper boundary of a P-shaped profile, a period of equilibrium often ensues, characterised by a balance between buyers and sellers. The lower portion of this profile takes on a long and slender shape, symbolising a limited trading volume. Conversely, the broader upper section signifies the attainment of a 'fair' price and a surge in trading activity. P-shaped patterns are typically construed as bullish indicators.

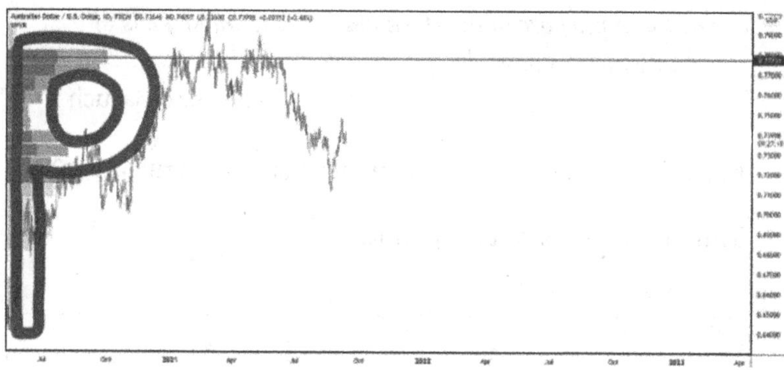

Next, you have a b-shaped profile: b-shaped volume profiles take shape when a market experiences a sharp decline followed by consolidation. Unlike the P-shaped profiles, b-shaped volume profiles often emerge after an extended consolidation phase.

While P-shaped profiles typically signify short covering, b-shaped profiles indicate a phase of selling activity before equilibrium is re-established in the market. The elongated and slender upper portion of a b-shaped profile reflects lower trading volume and a perception of price that may be deemed 'unfair'. In contrast, the broader lower section signifies the point at which the price finally balances buyers and sellers. Commonly associated with downtrends, when b-shaped profiles appear during an uptrend, they can potentially signal a reversal. Since b-shaped profiles suggest long positions are exiting the market, they are generally considered bearish indicators.

In addition to both P and b shapes, other profiles in volume terms include D and Capital B.

D-shaped volume profiles materialise when a momentary equilibrium prevails within a market. The Point of Control (PoC) typically resides at the profile's centre, signifying a state of equilibrium where neither buyers nor sellers display heightened aggression. Nevertheless, discerning order flow traders who exercise patience may seek out D-shaped volume profiles, envisioning the potential for a dual-direction breakout as institutional participants fortify their positions.

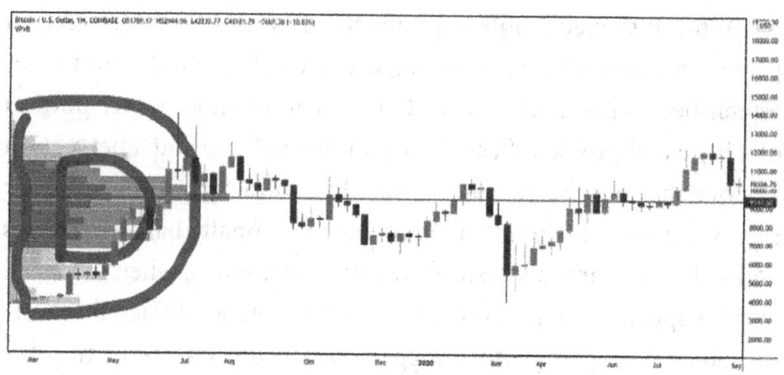

Capital B-shaped volume profiles emerge when two D-shaped profiles unfold within a defined timeframe. Although a single value area and PoC are present, specific order flow traders divide the profile into two separate D-shaped regions, each with its distinct value area. While Capital B-shaped profiles are typically seen as a trend continuation, it's crucial to ascertain the dominant PoC, indicating whether the heightened activity occurred at the upper or lower section of the profile.

You can spot these profiles without the need for indicators. While adding the indicators does not harm you, your eyes will be drawn to them. Once you see them, you are unable to un-see them. Each pattern has a different story; when combining the story with your existing bias, you start to see how powerful these techniques can be.

Overall, it takes a little bit of common sense, but if you can approach a chart and spot volume or lack of volume, price movements already painted, it's fantastic when your eyes can see a naked chart. You're able to give an up or down bias almost instantly. Some of what I say here might come across as very repetitive or even boring. But trust me, it's here by design. I've coached enough traders to know what parts need to be discussed and hammered home.

Again, I want to summarise what you might not realise you now know. If you can see a naked chart and visualise your Elliott Wave bias, you can quickly determine if we are in a markup, markdown or sideways phase. Spotting thin or chunky volume will give hints on top of the Elliott Wave count as to where next. You can spot lower timeframe master pattern areas. You can now add volume profile shapes that will only enhance your read on the chart and the overall situation. You also know that more volume is pumped in at certain times of the day over the different trading sessions. And why does the Composite Man do this to control the price when he finishes the accumulation or distribution?

See where you have come thus far! . . .

CHAPTER 11

CONSOLIDATIONS

'Do not anticipate and move without market confirmation. Being a little late in your trade is your insurance that you are right or wrong.'

—Jesse Livermore

https://www.fullertonmarkets.com/blog/top-10-trading-rules-by-great-trader-jesse-livermore-part

As you may have noticed, the markets exhibit various patterns and behaviours. This is how we can spot things like Elliott Wave counts or Wyckoff schematics. As I mentioned in Chapter 9, consolidation ranges play a pivotal role, primarily due to the market being in some consolidation state most of the time.

Understanding consolidation ranges is essential. In this chapter I want to cover consolidation ranges, exploring what they are and why they occur.

People often use various terminology for a consolidation range, referred to as a trading range or congestion area, which is a period in the market when the price of an asset moves within a relatively narrow range, characterised by a lack of a clear trend in either direction.

During this phase, the market appears to be in equilibrium, with neither buyers nor sellers exerting significant dominance. After reading the previous chapters, you already know otherwise. Consolidation ranges can be observed on various timeframes, from minutes to weeks or even months, depending on the context.

Why do consolidation ranges occur?

The answer is for several reasons. Accumulation and distribution mainly. Consolidation results from large institutional traders accumulating or distributing their positions. They enter the market discreetly, causing the price to remain within a range until they decide to initiate a new trend. Or, as I said earlier, this is before the markup or markdown.

Another reason they can happen is simply market indecision, when we get a period of uncertainty or indecision among market participants. Traders may wait for significant news, economic data or events before coming out in a clear direction. Although I still prefer to think Composite Man has yet to fill his boots or sell all his products.

In other instances, this could be a slowing down of activity at the end of the Asian session or coming into a weekend close. Consolidation ranges are a natural part of market cycles, allowing brief pauses before resuming a trend.

In any scenario, the main thing to remember and keep an eye out for is what the range is most likely doing. Why is it here, and where did it come from?

A slow increase in the price throughout the Asian session is different from a significant markup during the New York session and into an expected pocket of liquidity, likely starting a distribution schematic.

You might, at times, see decreased volatility. During consolidation, volatility tends to decline, resulting in smaller price swings. This makes a master pattern on another timeframe, for example.

Note that trading volume typically decreases during consolidation, indicating reduced enthusiasm among traders. It is caused by uncertainty, exactly as Composite Man wants. You might wonder why I didn't cover this in an earlier chapter. The main reason is that you already have a good grasp of the logic behind a consolidation, so giving you why it happens before what you can do with it felt like an unnecessary step.

However, having this intel now means you can add to your understanding, knowing these areas go on to create 'areas of interest' or, as I call them, 'auction areas'. I am not entirely done with the auction areas yet; we will go deeper into them in the next chapter.

CHAPTER 12

AUCTION AREAS

'The market is a device for transferring money from the impatient to the patient.'

—Warren Buffet

https://www.pinterest.fr/pin/the-stock-market-is-a-device-for-transferring-money-from-the-impatient-to-the-patient-warren-buffett-inspirational--395050198542652447/

Above and beyond consolidation ranges, auction areas, as I like to call them, happen in several locations for many reasons. I have identified these as auction areas because, as a kid, I would go to auctions with my father. He would often buy and sell things, and we would go to auctions for machines and things for his engineering company. All I remember from the early days was learning how it worked, having the paddle, raising it to bid for an item, and that excitement when you won!

Trading, in general, is much the same: the entry, the disappointment when you lose and the thrill of winning!

But in terms of auction areas, I identify them as places where people go to buy and sell, as simple as that. You have to remember the market is often in a state of consolidation; this doesn't always mean these are auction areas.

I would look at a few things that I regard as auction areas, areas of interest for potential action in the future. These consolidation zones will create some auction areas, and various other candlestick patterns can make different types of auction areas.

As Chapters 9 and 11 suggest, these areas are where people come to trade. Suppose you can visualise these zones as an auction house. You will have buyers and sellers competing for the price to go in their favour, but more than this, you have orders above and below that may or may not get triggered during the next swing. This is often why the price is pulled back to these areas; usually, the price goes just beyond before being rejected violently again in the initial direction. Take a look at this example.

I have identified an auction area represented by the line in this image. The price comes down and rejects to the upside, then comes back and rejects a second time before returning a third time.

As you can see in the image, as the price returns a third time, it accelerates from the underside and substantially changes character. This is making higher highs above the previous two highs.

The cause is the untapped liquidity sitting below the auction area.

It's never as easy as saying, 'Here's an auction area; it will do x'. Unfortunately, there's a lot more to it than that.

Knowing where to look is a good start. You can drill down the timeframes and try to look for clues, but in the grand scheme of things you don't need that level of insight to be a profitable trader. If you're curious, go for it.

Some YouTube influencers and educators will refer to this as the 'Smart Money' concept. You will hear things like order blocks and imbalances. Some less informed traders will still talk about support and resistance.

Neither is wrong; it is simply different terminology. The market always seeks liquidity and will always go after supply or demand. It isn't any more complex than that.

If you look at the previous image again, you can see the price played back to the level, and on the second attempt, the high was lower than the high before, thus making lower lows and lower highs. In 99% of trading manuals, you expect the market to make new lows and continue the downtrend.

In this image, we can see lower highs and lows formed, and then as the market makes the third low, it rallies.

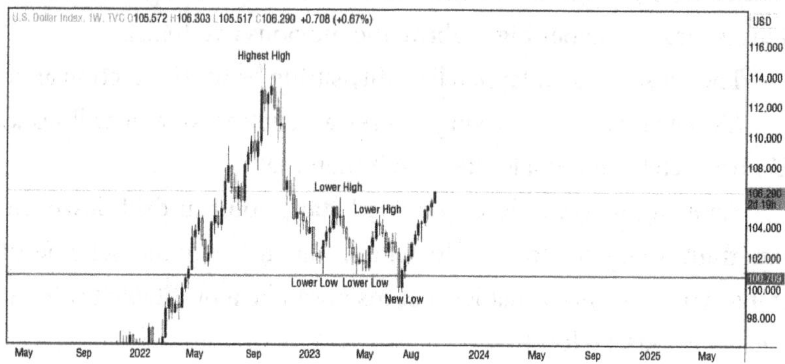

This is the perfect example of trapping traders to the downside and taking stops directly after people who entered short at the first lower high and second lowest high marked in the image.

This example is even more interesting because it's now moving on to do something else. Take a look at the next image.

This image shows a consolidation marked with a box.

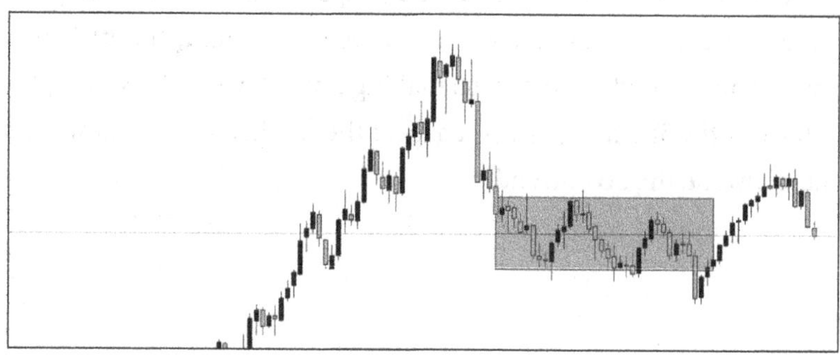

The box on a weekly timeframe shows the tightening of the price. What about zooming out and seeing the monthly chart? I will keep the box on for reference.

Monthly view of the same weekly chart.

What it's doing is making a new auction area slightly higher than before. Think of the Elliott Wave counting technique (see Chapter 16 later); the one must move impulsively, and the two can't come lower than the starting point.

So, if we draw a 50% line on the box and extend it to the right, we should see a pullback seeking liquidity before the price moves up. The levitations would be regarded as two up to three.

With an extended 50% marker.

How does this look down on the weekly?

The zoomed-in view highlights two key facts.

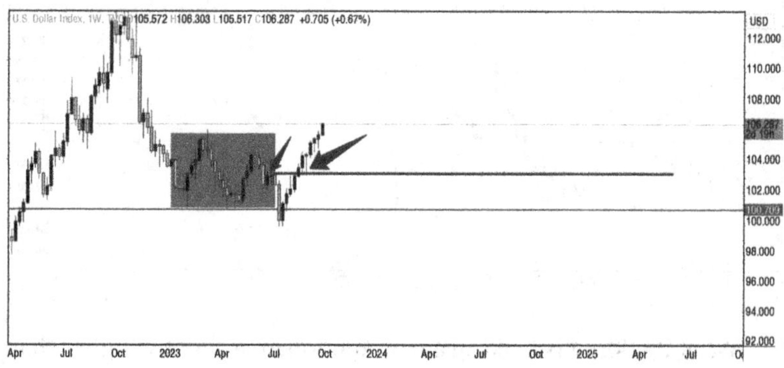

When zoomed back in, you can see that the arrow on the left shows a minor consolidation inside the more significant move, meaning if you zoom in on the daily, you will have a box inside the box.

The second arrow shows how the price rallied through the 50% marker but returned precisely to it as a re-test before continuing.

Here's something else of interest.

This image shows the price now; the expansion below equals 100% and the equilibrium is the 50% marker.

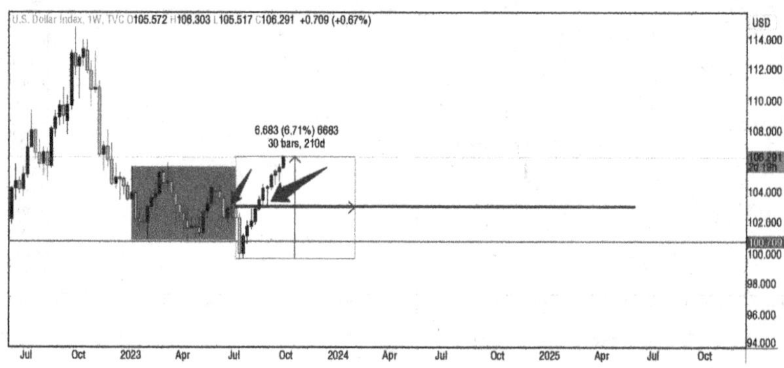

These aren't just examples found from looking through countless charts; these are live and current as I write this book. I have covered this move in some of my TradingView streams, which, of course, is also an immutable ledger to show you how these things play out in the future.

Other elements that constitute auction areas, although probably not quite as powerful as the consolidation zone example above, are due to the several ways in which auction areas are formed.

The most common would be the reversal candles of a swing; the last buy candle before the trend reverses and starts its descent, or the complete inverse. The previous sell candle before the price begins to rally. I like to call these 'buy before you sell' and 'sell before you buy'.

In the previous images, you will see a strong down candle (the lowest low) on the weekly timeframe, followed by the sequence of up candles. Liquidity is sat here as well. This is a kind of indecision area whereby buyers drove the price up, but sellers fought hard to keep the momentum going down. There will, of course, be liquidity under the low. But this is where the support comes in. We tapped liquidity twice before forming this candle pattern. Nothing is saying we can't tap into it again in the future.

If you look at the image on the next page, you will see, at a glance, the areas of high and low volume marked here in freehand. This is what I see instinctively when assessing a chart; I want you to think the same way.

I have drawn a rough volume profile based on what I am seeing. There is good volume up high as we had an apparent reversal; the central area from the swing low to the swing high is probably around my two lines. Then, under my line, you will see what is known as an imbalance. I'll explain this next. Under that, you have the following sideways action before the lowest spike in volume, which was the liquidity for this move up.

So, as rudimentary as this seems, what I am doing here is giving by eye the idea that I feel the price needs to come back after a rally to test the liquidity made at the 50% marker, then travel up to the higher zones before losing its momentum and coming back to seek lower levels of liquidity.

If you zoom in on the smaller timeframes, you will see smaller consolidation patterns on the reversal candles; remember, that's just a Wyckoff schematic. You can't be bothered to go and assess on that small level as you know what's next.

Imbalances refer to a situation in markets, particularly in stock or securities trading, forex and commodities, where a significant disparity exists between the supply and demand for a particular asset. This imbalance can occur for various reasons. But all it means is that the price shot through a level, and there was no interest from the other party at that stage.

This image highlights an imbalance.

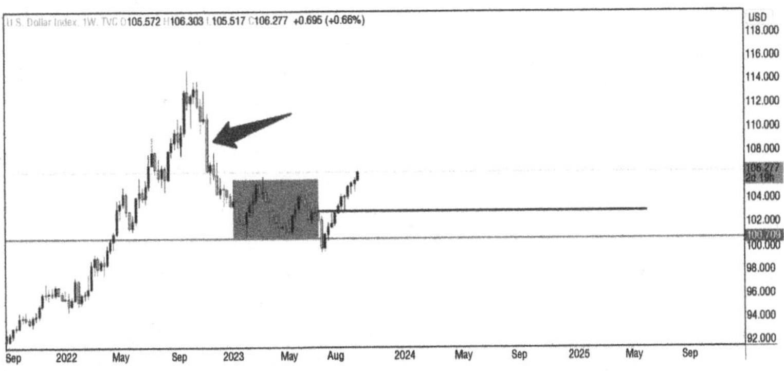

As you can see above, the arrow shows a down candle whereby the price has yet to cover it; the market moves up and down, and what you tend to find is that the price drops in the next candle or two. The price comes back, in essence, covering the price to the left. Please think of this logically; it is simply grabbing liquidity as it flows. However, in this instance, it dropped and did not return to the same level (yet). This type of move could be an ideal or even a primary target, with the secondary upside target being the auction area at the previous high. You see how it fits together, always chasing new liquidity. I will cover the imbalance effect more in the next chapter, but it was essential to give you a view here as it's all part of the same 'auction area' identification.

Once you can start putting the chapters together, they should merge. It all comes back to assessing a naked chart and knowing where and why liquidity sits, where it sits.

CHAPTER 13

INTERESTING AREAS

What I have covered in the last few chapters leads to this term I frequently use: 'interesting areas'. People often want to find a line or a price point. Imagine the level of accuracy you would need to pinpoint a line in price. Again, visualise these lines weeks or even months in advance.

Other educators will all have their lingo for such areas; some will call these areas 'order blocks', some talk about it as 'Wyckoff', others refer to it as a 'master pattern', and probably a load more. The truth is, they are all the same thing—illustrated differently. All you need to know is why they happen and how to use them. This is easier than you might imagine. Most teachers will overcomplicate these things due to their lack of understanding, or pitch it to you as if it's some mythical silver bullet.

First things first: Why do you think a cluster happens in price?

Price consolidation in trading occurs when the market enters a period of relatively tight price range and reduced volatility after a trending move.

For example, after a significant price move, traders may become exhausted, leading to a temporary pause in the trend. This exhaustion can result from overbought or oversold conditions, and participants may need time to reassess their positions.

Or, after a substantial price move, traders who participated in the trend may decide to take profits. This profit-taking can contribute to a slowdown in the trend and lead to a period of consolidation. Hence, Wyckoff accumulation or distribution.

I hope you are now starting to piece some of these things together!

Without new information or catalysts to drive the market, participants may prefer to wait on the sidelines, reducing trading activity and price consolidation. Yet, if you have a good enough understanding of the bias, you can predict with great accuracy the direction of the next move away from these levels.

Understanding the reasons behind price consolidation is helpful. It can provide insights into potential future market movements, coupled with the more considerable bias—you are just refining your skills right here.

You have seen in earlier chapters examples of Wyckoff schematics, master patterns, consolidations and auction areas. It doesn't matter if you call them a box or an order block—it's the same thing.

There are a couple of crucial factors when analysing the charts.

Bias is essential, and a more considerable timeframe understanding of the Elliott cycle is needed to know if we are likely consolidating in an area of expected distribution (in this case, we go down next) or if we are in a zone or region of expected accumulation and more likely to go up.

You can also start looking at measuring these movements and forecast targets. To do this, see the following example.

In this image, you can see a consolidation marked with a box.

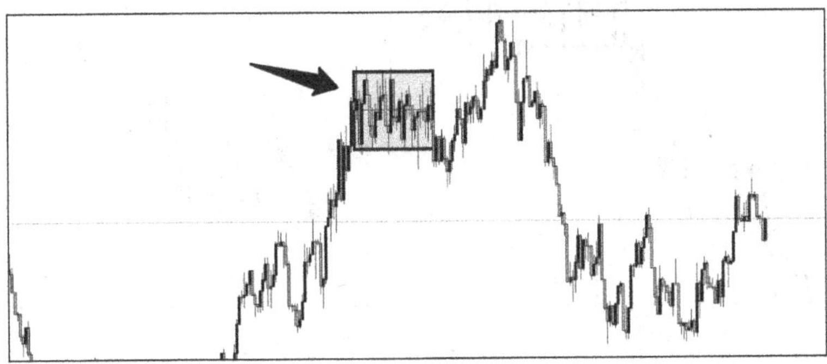

In the next image, you can see how the price breaks out and closes below the range; in other words, leaving the consolidation range.

Marked with an arrow and a line showing roughly the distance outside the range.

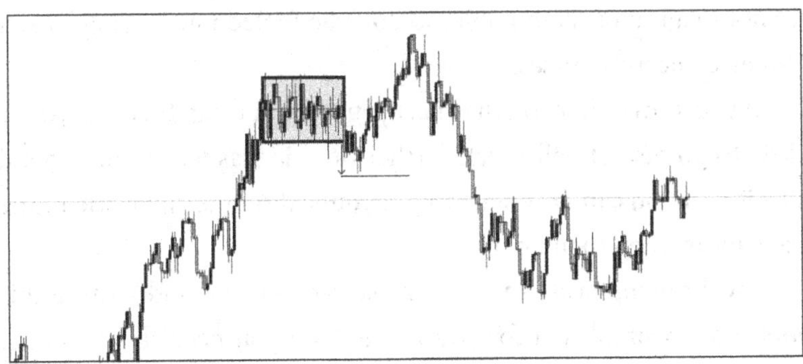

This is the region expansion; if you measure from the low to the high, you can see the move is nearly perfectly aligned with the 50% region of the consolidation.

This image shows the consolidation and expansion.

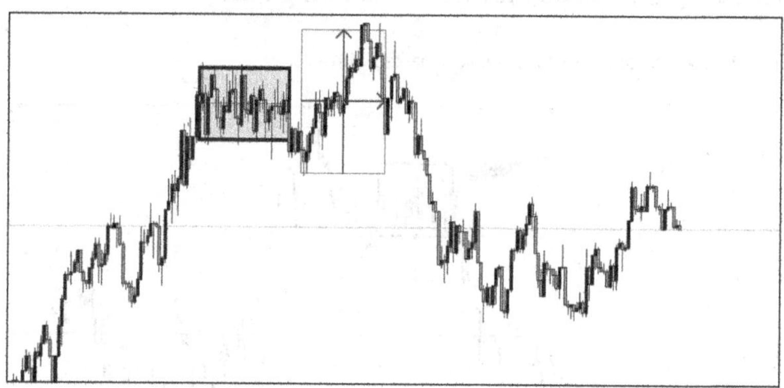

Look left, as they say. We can see, without much more evidence needed, that the price had been moving on up, making this region more likely exhausted at the top. Hence, we would expect a move down.

You will see these in every timeframe on every instrument. They are not magical or memorable, so don't be fooled into buying 'Smart Money Concept' courses.

If you know where on the chart you are and what direction you're likely to go next (I will touch further on this bias later), the general idea is that you can now start to put yourself on the right side of the trade more often than not.

I will re-emphasise that my whole rationale behind writing this book was to simplify it for you to the level you need to be trading professionally.

I wish I could say, 'forget everything you think you know about the market and see it in a simple format'. It constantly seeks liquidity, and although I have said 'it's an algorithm seeking liquidity', it's less of an algorithm and more of a sequence. When the market goes up, it must come down. Where is it likely to come down? Well, liquidity pools, of course. It would be best if you viewed it as this simple.

Many new traders get caught in the trap of trying to be perfect—perfect levels, perfect entries, believing they need to see swing highs and lows. They tend to overcomplicate it by looking for too much. Too many indicators, too many instruments, too many timeframes. Yet, there is not enough logic.

If you understand that the market breathes, after a long sprint it will recover; if it's going further, you can identify that in advance, wait for the recovery time and go again.

I have been fighting myself here not to put too many illustrations into this book—visualising precisely what I am saying will help you remove the 'textbook' examples that are never really textbook. Even zones like the last image I shared are subjective. Do you go from the wicks, just the bodies? Where does it start?

The answer, well, there is no correct answer. It's a matter of testing it on various instruments and timeframes. Make notes and test it some more. You will soon find character traits. This is the foundation, not the textbook.

CHAPTER 14

IMBALANCE

'The way to learn to do things is to do things. The way to learn a trade is to work at it. Success teaches how to succeed. Begin with the determination to succeed, and the work is half done already.'

—Henry Ford

https://quotepark.com/quotes/1431785-henry-ford-the-way-to-learn-to-do-things-is-to-do-things-the/

As you already know from the previous chapter, imbalance levels are part of interesting areas. I wanted to add a chapter delving more into the imbalances because it will help you see the larger-scale picture around liquidity.

I discussed volume profile shapes earlier, as well as how Wyckoff mastered patterns and translated them as part of the consolidation ranges. Well, imbalance areas are almost the opposite; these are thin volumes. Imagine a repetitive volume profile shape on the chart when you see the price dropping from a high and moving down into a cluster at a low.

You would have a lowercase 'b', and the inverse is true if the price was to move from a base up to a high and consolidate. You would then have a 'P' shape. Do you see where I am going with this?

Many people fail to realise that the candles or the timeframe they view have information inside them. So, if we are viewing a 4-hour chart, the 15-minute volume profile will be inside in detail. The 4-hour candle might only be a long wick and volume on the bottom or top.

The point is that you have candle stories that can be extracted on the one side, zooming in, and then the 4-hour candle you are viewing creates part of a story on the higher timeframes such as the daily or the weekly.

Thin volume can give plenty of information and opportunities. The algorithm is often attracted back to these areas; the volume is slim, so the price can easily break through the zone. So, if the gap is filled, it's likely to continue until the next auction area with some sizable liquidity inside. Consider them like anomalies, representing points on a price chart with a significant disparity between buying and selling activity. They emerge when one side of the market, either buyers (bulls) or sellers (bears), exerts dominance over the other, resulting in price movement that deviates from the norm.

Teachers and online gurus have other names for these areas, such as 'fair value gaps', yet it's the same thing. While the consolidation shows lots of activity in a tight range, an imbalance is displaying how the price shot through the area with such force that it didn't allow the opposition to have orders filled. Technically, they are very similar to auction areas, so they would also fit under the 'interesting areas' umbrella.

Imbalances can happen on all timeframes, from intraday charts to daily, weekly or monthly charts. Imbalance areas are not limited to any specific trading asset, making them a versatile concept applicable across various financial markets, including stocks, futures and forex.

What types of imbalance areas are there?

A single price level has a disproportionately high volume of either buying or selling activity, creating an imbalance. This often results in a gap on the price chart as the market moves quickly away from that level.

Range extension imbalances are another kind and can occur when a market breaks out of a well-defined trading range with significant force. This indicates a sudden shift in sentiment, usually driven by a major news event or a shift in market dynamics.

In *Master the Art of Trading*, I talked about candle stories where the candles display different volumes than the candle itself. You're looking for areas where the volume is skewed heavily to one side, indicating an imbalance.

Gaps in price charts are often indicative of an imbalance. A gap occurs when the market opens significantly higher or lower than the previous day's close.

Another thing to note is that imbalanced areas often transform into support or resistance zones over bigger timeframes.

I like that they can confirm the continuation of an existing trend. If a market experiences an imbalance in the direction of the prevailing trend, this suggests that the trend is likely to persist. Think of what I showed in Chapter 12: the price is expected to seek liquidity one way, then flow through the imbalance, filling it to the next area of interest.

Range extension imbalances are particularly relevant for breakout traders. When an imbalance results in a breakout from a consolidation phase, it can offer a high-reward trading opportunity.

Leveraging imbalanced areas in trading requires a systematic approach and well-defined strategies. While imbalance areas offer valuable insights, they are not foolproof signals. Not all imbalances result in significant price moves. Some may fizzle out, leading to false signals.

You can easily fall into the trap of overusing historical imbalance areas, which may not always play out the same way in the future. Once they are used, deem them invalid.

Shifts in imbalances can happen rapidly due to changes in market sentiment, news events or external factors.

So, what does this look like on a chart?

In this image, going from the top down, the first example arrow just below swings high.

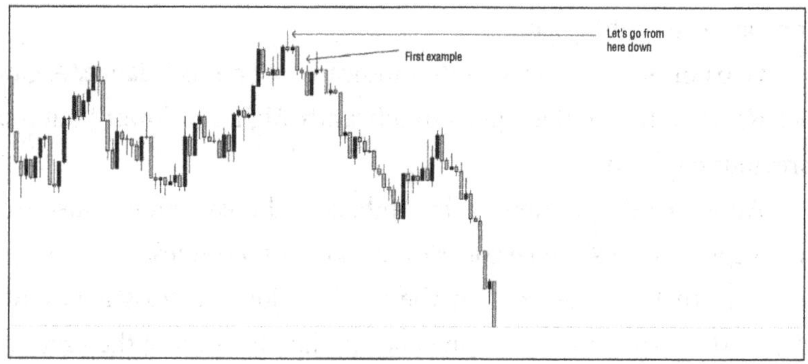

If you imagine three candles, you have one before, the central candle and one after.

The example above shows the swing high followed by a little green candle immediately after. Then, a large red candle with a much larger body. A tiny red candle follows this.

So, if we take the low of the candle before and the high of the candle after, we have a thin volume in that space.

This is a zoomed-in version of the previous illustration.

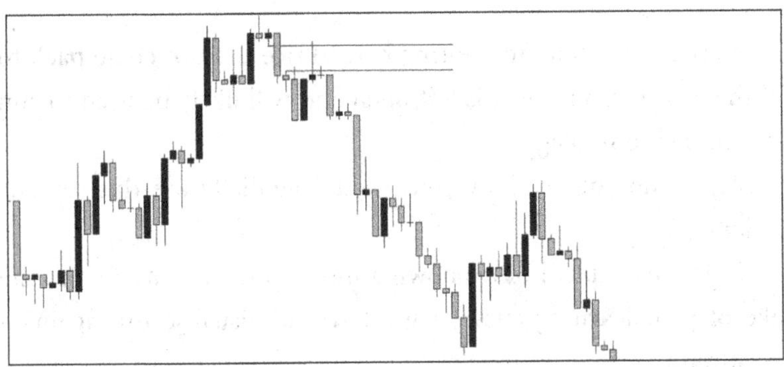

As you can see, the candles are low before and high after, and I have marked them with lines to the right. Price will likely fill this gap (fuel to move down).

Looking at the next candle after the third (top after the central candle), you can see the price enter the zone and drop further. Then, two candles later, it entered the zone again and continued filling the gap before dropping further down.

In the next image, you will see the next gap formed.

This image shows the next imbalance gap formed.

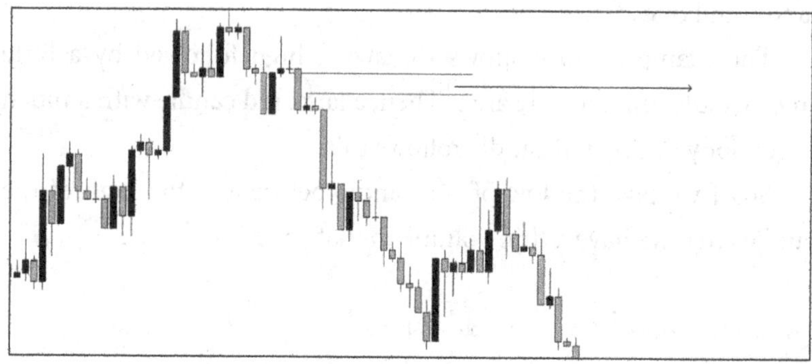

Notice something interesting here? Price did not come back to fill the gap. This means it is left open and will likely be used to run back into at some stage.

Again, do you see how you could potentially use this to your advantage?

In this example, I have shown a move to the downside. For the sake of your learning curve, I want you to visualise this again in an uptrend.

Before reading on, take a minute or two to think logically about this. What would you expect to see as the difference?

. . .

I hope you did take the time to give that some thought, as I will not put another image here.

In an upward example, you should think about the candle before, the central candle and the candle after.

Now, starting from the candle before, we can draw a line from the top (it's high), then through the central candle and the following line would be at the candle's low to the right of the central candle. These two lines show the gap.

Take your time; search for a couple of these on various charts. You will see them in every timeframe and on every instrument.

Of course, the bigger the timeframe, the more emphasis they will have. You now have some pretty valuable tools and knowledge at your disposal. At this stage in the book, you should have a good idea of all the essential 'interesting areas', why they are exciting and how to spot them.

I cannot stress enough the importance of testing, visualising and using TradingView's bar reply tool—play with it, test it and test it some more. For example, you can squeeze the candles up tight using the bar reply tool to avoid cheating. Return to some random date and then scale the chart around. Now draw these levels, both consolidations and imbalances. Before clicking play, zoom out and put a bias on your chart. You will start to see why the price will go up or down. You will begin to notice that the market sequence is searching for liquidity. Your Elliott count will give you a clue as to where you are in the bigger picture. This way, when you click the forward or the play button, you will already have your areas of interest lined up.

Prepare to be AMAZED.

would be at the church, below the point of the central candle. These two lines show the path.

Take your time, search for a complete set of these on various churches. You'll see them in each church and on most illustrations.

Of course I'd suggest [illegible] make most emphasis they will have [illegible] [illegible] of this stage in the [illegible] should have [illegible] [illegible] [illegible] [illegible] [illegible].

[illegible]

CHAPTER 15

POINT OF CONTROL

What I want to do in this chapter is cover something I know many people cannot see or piece together. Everything I have covered in the last few chapters brings us to volume.

Think about it—thin volume of the imbalance areas, heavy volume of the consolidation ranges . . . and the penny drops.

You know I told you these things happen on every timeframe? Well, now get this: a smaller timeframe accumulation or distribution schematic will resemble the consolidation box on a slightly higher timeframe. Think about it.

If you imagine drawing a box on the higher timeframe chart, zoom in and look inside. If you were to draw a volume profile inside the box, you would see volume active inside that. Which means it will show some interesting data. See the image below.

An example of volume inside a range.

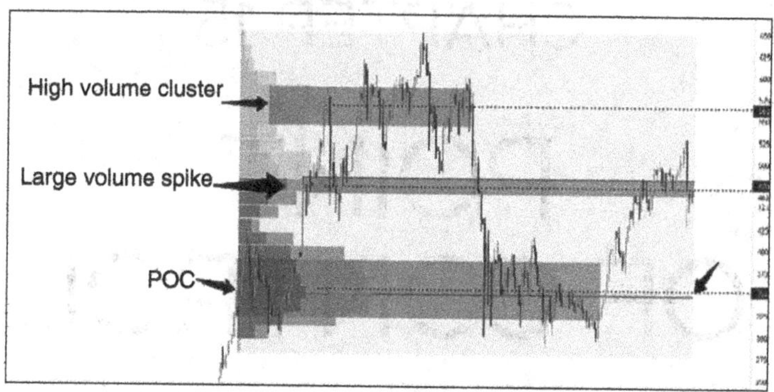

As this image shows, you might find a cluster; this will be the Point of Control (PoC). Now think back to Chapter 10.

The above shows that the volume is heavily weighted to the lower part of the drawing. This is the volume PoC.

The gap between this PoC and the significant volume spike above would be deemed as low volume or thin volume, with another high-volume cluster above that again. So, in essence, what we are seeing here is from top to bottom.

From the top spike in volume is a thin volume into a high-volume cluster—likely a consolidation on a smaller timeframe; from there down, we have a gap otherwise known as an imbalance or fair value gap. Then there is a spike in volume—how about you think of this as a cluster area—followed by a thin volume or gap, down to the more significant cluster PoC.

See, it's not all that difficult.

Do you want another surprise? Take the volume profile off and drop down a timeframe.

When you do this on the chart, draw a box around the consolidation levels and draw lines or rectangles to highlight the thin volume between your consolidation zones. Now, go back to a higher timeframe! Boom, same intel and no indicator!

Trading is all about giving yourself an edge; you don't need to be correct 100% of the time to be profitable. It would be best if you had a bias and some simple logic. If this is added to proper risk management, you are now likely to be on the right side of a trade more often than not. Statistically speaking, you're now a profitable trader over time.

This chapter was a short one. I want to touch on some other points and return to this theory when you have built up your understanding over the following few chapters.

CHAPTER 16

ELLIOTT WAVES

'Forces travel in waves, as demonstrated by Galileo, Newton and other scientists.'

—Ralph Nelson Elliott

https://thecitesite.com/authors/ralph-nelson-elliott/

More often than not, people tend to overcomplicate the Elliott Wave Theory. With what I have covered here and the more in-depth breakdown in *Master the Art of Trading*, I want to show you just how simple you can make it.

This image shows an Elliott Wave count (0–5) inside wave 1, then the (ABC) of wave two and up.

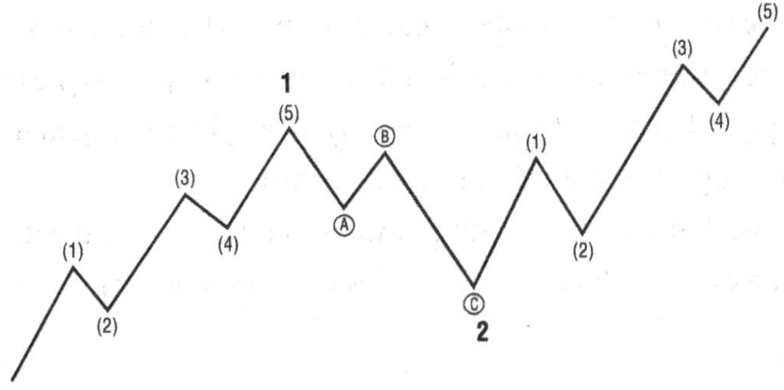

The reality is that this is nearly as much as you need to understand. The market is seeking liquidity; as the price rallies and pulls back on the minor wave, it creates liquidity in the form of imbalances and interesting areas.

I have read somewhere—don't quote me on where—that if you ask 10 Elliottitions for their count, you will get 11 different answers!

If you can visualise the logic behind these moves, you will be doing alright.

So, step by step, the first thing you need to know is that there are only three golden rules.

1. Wave 3 is never the shortest.
2. Wave 2 never goes below 0.
3. Wave 4 does not overlap into the zone 1 territory.

Pretty simple, right?

What I want you to do now is think of the logic behind each of these golden rules.

Why is wave 3 never the shortest? Wave 3 is deemed the most impulsive move. When you look inside it, you will see the larger operators Composite Man has had time to sell off positions in on the way down, start accumulation and push up from 0 to 1. Now, as the price comes back from 1 to 2 and then back again, you will obviously have the stop losses of traders who went short at 1; new entries short as the price seems to make a double top at precisely the same level as the high of 1. Then, of course, new buyers will be coming in to push the price up. Hence, it is impulsive by nature.

If the 0 to 1 wave were longer, we would be capping the distance that waves 3 and 5 could travel. If wave 5 were longer, Composite

Man would have less profit due to a worse entry point. This last statement is only partially true. It will help you think of it more logically. There is nothing saying wave 1 or wave 5 can't be the shortest or the longest. But you would expect wave 3, more often than not. In addition, assume wave 1 is, let's say, 100 pips, wave 3 is 150 pips and wave 5 is 180 pips. We have not broken the number one golden rule—wave 1 is the shortest; wave 3 is the second longest.

What about rule two? Picture the logic: What does it mean if wave 2 should enter the 'liquidity' region below the base of the move from 0 to 1? It would invalidate the psychology of the whole move as now, technically, we have a new low. It's pretty simple when you think of it like that, isn't it?

Rule three is pretty similar to rule two. But instead of making a new low, the logic behind it—not going below the high of wave 1—is all about who controls the move. If there are stops and new positions ready to short there, the larger operators run the risk of losing control if it were to drop too far. This is why wave 4 is often a slow, drawn-out process.

In addition to the golden rules, Elliott Wave Theory has a set of guidelines for corrective moves; they range from Fibonacci relationships to the types of waves.

The issue for me is that this is more complex than it needs to be. Once you have a grasp of the larger wave count, you will begin to notice relationships. For example, after a sizeable impulsive move, like the image at the start of this chapter, the price tends to come back deep for wave 2. You often see pullbacks beyond the 61.8% (a standard ratio, in Fibonacci terms).

I could write a whole book on Elliott Wave Theory. But much like the rest of this book, my goal is to simplify the process for you.

I would say that impulsive moves tend to be in wave 5 and corrective in wave 3—hence, up 0 to 5 and down A, B and C.

With the three golden rules and now thinking of the logic behind why these moves happen anyway, you have enough to obtain a bias.

CHAPTER 17

FOOTPRINT INDICATOR

'The forces that cause market trends have their origin in nature and human behavior.'

—Ralph Nelson Elliott

https://thecitesite.com/authors/ralph-nelson-elliott/

Thinking back to Chapter 15, for you to understand how this has an impact on the price movement, you need to go one layer deeper. This is where footprints come in.

To effectively analyse footprint charts, you must understand their essential elements, such as volume bars, buy and sell imbalances and the bid–ask spread. Each element contributes to understanding market dynamics and can reveal hidden trading opportunities.

Delving further into the volume and volume profile realm, the next level of understanding involves examining the volume within the market and individual candlesticks.

Footprint charts, Depth of Market (DOM) and Delta analysis are interconnected concepts. Footprint charts, a variation of candlestick charts, offer additional insights beyond price movement by incorporating trade volume and order flow data. This elevates the analysis beyond merely considering the asset's price. This tool is gaining in popularity, especially among charting software providers.

Order flow and DOM, while containing similar information, present it differently. Both order flow and DOM represent the buy and sell orders in the market. DOM assesses the supply and demand for tradable assets based on open buy and sell orders for assets like stocks or futures contracts. A higher quantity of these orders characterises a more profound or liquid market.

This data is often called the order book, listing pending orders for a security or currency. It is pivotal in determining which transactions can be executed and the total volume bought or sold by navigating the order book to a specific price level.

DOM is frequently displayed as an electronic roster of outstanding buy and sell orders, categorised by price level and constantly updated to mirror current market activity. A matching engine pairs compatible trades to facilitate their completion.

The Delta footprint illustrates the net contrast at each price point between the volume initiated by buyers and that created by sellers. It aids traders in validating the commencement and continuity of a price trend.

In summary, these tools offer a glimpse inside each candle, revealing the number and types of orders, among other details. Combined, they provide a comprehensive view of orders, their nature and their discrepancies. This broad perspective can be advantageous, particularly for shorter-term, scalp-style trades, granting a subtle advantage over more conventional candlestick and line charts.

Below is an example of a footprint chart featuring the Delta analysis at the bottom.

https://www.whselfinvest.com/en-nl/trading/want/broker-comparison/34-ATAS
This image shows the footprint chart, including the CVD below.

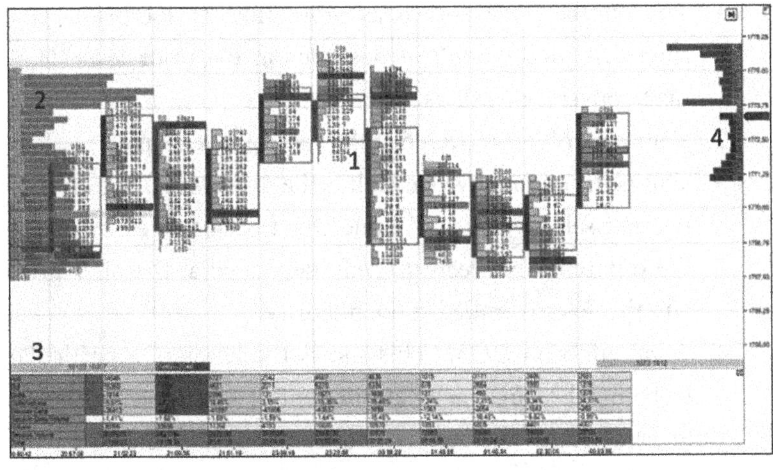

Why is this relevant? It's helpful to understand, but you almost don't need this level of detail.

Well, why did I include it?

I chose to put this here so you can dig deep into the psychology that creates the movements in price action. The numbers inside the candles become apparent when you drop timeframes and draw boxes and imbalances. If you want to support it, switch on footprint charts.

Do you need it? 100% NO!!!

Market Footprint, DOM and Delta

To help you understand, I labelled the previous chart to give insight into what you could see. You will notice numbers next to the candles, but they are still red and green.

1. The numbers are known as order flow or footprint. This shows the order book of positions at the price level. How many buyers and sellers, in essence.
2. Volume profile as covered at the start of this chapter.
3. This is the cumulative Delta. It is the difference between buying and selling power. Volume Delta is calculated by taking the difference between the volume traded at the offer price and the volume traded at the bid price.
4. A variation on DOM. This shows the levels of a particular instrument being traded at different prices, allowing traders to understand the supply and demand and, therefore, the liquidity of the currency at each price point. A good DOM means that there will be good liquidity.

https://www.financemagnates.com/forex/technology/tradingview-adds-market-depth-feature/
This image shows the DOM in a little more detail.

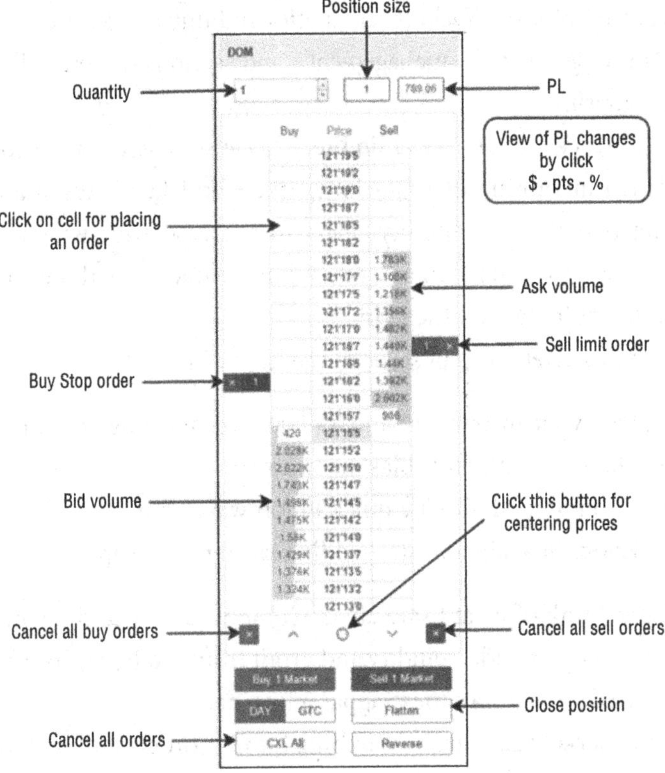

There's so much data here that it's easy for newer traders to confuse themselves. Hence, I wanted you to know these tools exist, but you can see all the information you need without them.

All you need to remember is that the market sequence is actively seeking liquidity. People often make this stuff complex; they make it hard on themselves for no reason. Brokers and exchanges throw RSI, MACD and moving averages at you. If you want to win in these markets, all you need to understand is where the liquidity sits and why it's searching one side more.

This is bias.

I've talked about Elliott, and you now know where master patterns, order blocks, Wyckoff schematics and imbalances are.

Apply good risk management, and seriously, you will surprise yourself.

The stock market seeks liquidity because it is essential for the efficient functioning of financial markets and facilitates smoother trading operations. Liquidity refers to the ease with which assets (such as stocks) can be bought or sold in the market without causing a significant impact on their prices.

Here's a brief recap of some of the key points.

- Pick your instrument and look at it from a long way out.
- Obtain a long-term bias up or down.
- Zoom in and give it a quick Elliott wave count.
- Zoom in again and start adding clusters and gaps.

Now, think of what I said about Composite Man and the market makers—they provide liquidity and profit from retail players who are unaware of how to spot these apparent points.

The market sequence is searching for new orders and stop losses. Where do retail traders place stops? At support and resistance levels. Why do we see expansions when talking about master patterns? Stop-loss hunting, of course.

It's comical when you break it down to the basics; sad for the retail traders, especially when they do not want to learn. You study 5 years or more to be a doctor or lawyer, yet they expect to watch a video on YouTube and become a professional money maker.

There's a saying along the lines of 'If you can't spot the liquidity, you are the liquidity'!

CHAPTER 18

LIQUIDITY

'Money flows, in effect, can render fundamental analysis futile in the short run, even while creating a compelling longer-term opportunity.'

—Seth Klarman

https://novelinvestor.com/quote-author/seth-klarman/

Liquidity is the lifeblood that courses through the veins of trading. It's the force that keeps markets vibrant, dynamic and capable of serving the needs of investors and traders alike. In this chapter, I aim to unravel the intricate tapestry of market liquidity, exploring how it works and how price tirelessly searches for it.

In its raw form, liquidity refers to the ease with which assets can be bought or sold in a market without significantly affecting their prices. Imagine a bustling marketplace where buyers and sellers gather to exchange goods. If there are plenty of participants, and they are willing to buy and sell freely, that market is considered liquid.

Conversely, a market with few participants or where they hesitate to trade is deemed illiquid.

Revisit Chapter 12. Think of how the interests of both buyers and sellers create liquidity.

An example of supply versus demand is if you had a one-of-a-kind car, let's say it's some vintage Ferrari. It's a one-off; the supply is limited, but the demand would be high so the price could get driven up by the lack of supply. This is an example of low liquidity.

The opposite would be true if someone were selling sand in Saudi Arabia. The demand would be low as it's accessible to most there; this also means the price would be driven down. So, whilst the sand is a wild example, tone this back a little and change the 'item' for something like gold or Bitcoin.

In both assets, there is supply; in both instruments, there is demand. Liquidity will change depending on the price and availability at that price.

The Two Sides of Market Liquidity

To grasp the intricacies of market liquidity, it is essential to understand the two sides of the liquidity coin: bid and ask.

Bid Liquidity. This represents the pool of willing buyers in the market. When you decide to sell an asset, you are essentially tapping into the bid liquidity. The more buyers there are at various price levels, the deeper the bid liquidity, and the easier it is to find a buyer at a desirable price.

Ask Liquidity. On the flip side is ask liquidity, the pool of willing sellers. When you wish to buy an asset, you interact with the ask liquidity. Deeper ask liquidity means you have a better chance of finding a seller at a favourable price.

The balance between bid and ask liquidity dictates the market's overall health. If there is an equilibrium between the two, it signifies a healthy and efficient market. However, an imbalance, where one side significantly outweighs the other, can lead to price gaps and excessive volatility.

The Mechanics of Market Liquidity

Market liquidity is not a static concept; it constantly evolves. Understanding its mechanics can show how it works and how price interacts with it.

Order Book. At the heart of market liquidity lies the order book. This real-time ledger displays all pending buy and sell orders for a particular asset. The order book is often divided into two sections: the bid side and the ask side.

- On the bid side, you see a list of buy orders with corresponding prices and quantities.
- On the ask side, you find sell orders with prices and quantities.

The order book is used to gauge market sentiment and assess the depth of liquidity at different price levels. It helps make informed decisions about when and at what price to enter or exit a trade.

Market Participants. Liquidity results from the collective actions of various market participants. These participants include individual retail traders, institutional investors, market makers and high-frequency trading firms. Each group contributes to the overall liquidity landscape in its unique way.

- Retail traders often provide liquidity by placing market orders and buying or selling assets at prevailing prices.

- Institutional investors, with their large trades, can absorb liquidity by executing substantial orders that might not be immediately matched.
- Market makers play a crucial role by constantly quoting bid and ask prices, ensuring there is always some level of liquidity available in the market.
- High-frequency trading firms engage in algorithmic trading to profit from minor price discrepancies and, in the process, contribute to liquidity provision.

Volatility and Liquidity. Liquidity and price volatility share an intricate relationship. High liquidity tends to dampen price swings, while low liquidity can exacerbate them. When there is an influx of market orders or a sudden news event, liquidity can evaporate, leading to price gaps and rapid price changes.

How Price Hunts for Liquidity

Price discovery is the process by which asset prices find equilibrium in the market. It's a continuous tug-of-war between buyers and sellers, and liquidity plays a pivotal role in this dance.

Tapping into the Order Book. When a trader or investor places an order in the market, they are essentially tapping into the existing order book. If they place a market order, they will be matched with the best available prices in the order book, instantly consuming liquidity.

Price Impact. Large orders have the potential to move the market. As buyers or sellers exhaust the available liquidity at a particular price level, they may need to transact at less favourable prices as they move further into the order book. This phenomenon is known as price impact.

Slippage. This occurs when a trade is executed at a price different from the expected price due to a lack of liquidity. It can happen during periods of high volatility or when dealing with illiquid assets.

Hunting for Hidden Liquidity. Traders employ various strategies to pursue hidden liquidity. For instance, they may use iceberg orders, which only display a portion of the total order size, keeping the rest hidden to avoid impacting the market too significantly.

Impact on Trading Strategies. Liquidity considerations influence trading strategies. For example, in highly liquid markets, traders might opt for high-frequency strategies that capitalise on small price movements. In contrast, they may adopt a more patient, long-term approach in illiquid markets.

Factors Affecting Market Liquidity

Market liquidity is not constant, it ebbs and flows in response to a myriad of factors. Here are some key determinants.

Market Hours. Liquidity often follows market hours. Assets traded in different time zones will experience varying levels of liquidity depending on the time of day. Liquidity tends to be highest during market hours when participants are most active.

Asset Type. Different types of assets exhibit varying levels of liquidity. For example, major currency pairs in the forex market are highly liquid, while thinly traded stocks may be illiquid.

Economic Events. Economic releases, earnings reports and geopolitical events can significantly impact liquidity. Traders often brace for increased volatility and potential liquidity shortages during such events.

Market Sentiment. Sentiment can sway liquidity. Bullish sentiment can lead to a rush of buyers, increasing liquidity on the bid side, while bearish sentiment can do the opposite.

Regulatory Changes. Regulatory changes can alter the market's liquidity landscape. For instance, introducing new rules or regulations can impact the behaviour of market participants and, consequently, liquidity.

Now, let's dig a little deeper. There are two different types of liquidity you should be aware of.

Inside Liquidity. Inside liquidity considers the gap between a swing high to low or a swing low to high. This could be anything we discussed in earlier chapters, such as auction areas or master patterns.

Inside liquidity is often chased on smaller timeframes after a breach of outside liquidity. Think of where new orders and old stops are likely sitting.

Outside Liquidity. Outside liquidity refers to the ability to execute a trade by moving the market with a large order that goes beyond the existing bid and ask prices. Or, in other words, outside the local high or low-swing extremes.

Here's an image to help you visualise the difference.

This image shows a local swing high and a swing low (outside) liquidity (inside being the gap).

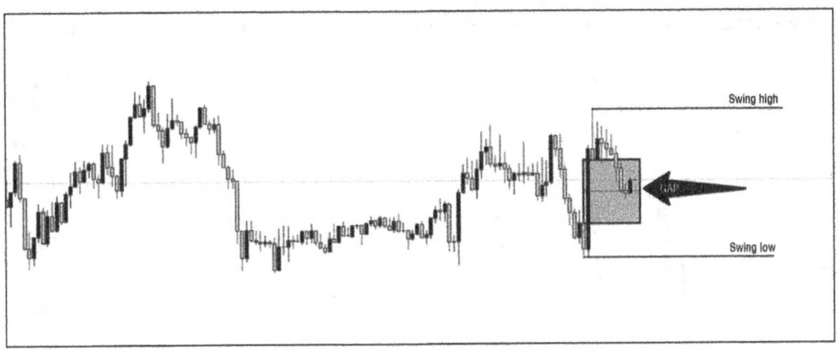

If the price has recently swept an extreme, assume it recently took liquidity from a swing low to fuel the move up. The chances are it might have left some form of gap. This would be deemed inside liquidity as we have yet to sweep the outside liquidity above. So, in this example, you could anticipate a move back down into the gap (clearing inside liquidity), then fuelling the move up to sweep potentially the outside liquidity above.

Think of it like the market needs to grab liquidity one way to go and move the opposite way. Once it has collected new orders and stop losses, it's likely to accelerate the other way. It is this that causes the waves and these are broken down into motive and pullback waves.

There's a perfect example of this happening right now in the Bitcoin chart as I write this, on 28 February 2024. We see the liquidity sat up higher, in addition to the retail sentiment that seems to be up only. In Chapter 20 I will cover COT data and when you combine this with retail sentiment, as well as knowing exactly where liquidity sits, it is beyond obvious. Let me share with you the chart and the COT snapshot. All you need to see on that image is long or short.

In this image, you can see the volume on the right and the liquidity levels of both outside zones.

CHAPTER 19

SUPPLY AND DEMAND

'Liquidity does not exist unless someone else is willing to give you cash in exchange for the piece of paper you want to sell.'

—Peter Bernstein

https://novelinvestor.com/quote-author/peter-bernstein/

New traders often learn about basic trading techniques, including support and resistance and supply and demand. Babypips.com defines supply and demand as follows.

Supply and Demand

Supply refers to the amount of an asset that is available, while demand is the quantity of an asset that people are willing to buy.
As the supply of an asset increases, its value declines. Conversely, as the supply of an asset decreases, its value rises. As demand for an asset increases, its value rises. Conversely, as demand for an asset decreases, its value declines.

> *Since this principle applies to the currency market, plenty of traders look at supply and demand for a particular currency at a given point in time to figure out whether that currency's value will rise or decline.*
>
> Source: https://www.babypips.com/forexpedia/supply-and-demand

The issue is that with this level of guidance, it is so much easier for someone new to trading not to grasp the concept.

Let me make this a little clearer for you. If you think of the term 'supply', the more supply we have, the more likely the price is to fall; contrary to that, the more demand we have, the more the price is expected to push up.

What happens if there is both supply and demand? Well, remember Chapter 9? What do you think causes the contraction phase? You could deem this an efficient market condition as, technically, we have enough buying and selling to keep the price at a level both parties seem to like.

Many don't seem to grasp the difference between support and resistance compared to supply and demand either. Supply and demand are areas whereby selling or buying is conducted, whereas support and resistance are the failure of price to reach beyond a level. Maybe it's just due to the fact that they sound similar—they get grouped more often than they should. They are not the same thing.

I want to show you now that you understand the term 'liquidity'. Think of supply and demand zones as a form of liquidity areas in the general sense.

The main thing to understand is that supply and demand are not created equal. Of course, external ranges such as swing highs and lows exist. Of course, these should be regarded as liquidity and a supply or demand zone, hence why they are bundled together for the most part.

However, supply and demand zones are also found inside the significant swing high and low areas I refer to as 'outside liquidity'. These are different from gaps, as gaps would be deemed inefficient market conditions because we see more buyers than sellers in an upward move and more sellers than buyers in a downward move.

To understand this, go back to visualising it and think about how a gap is created. Now, what would that look like in a smaller time-frame? It would simply look like an impulsive move. Consolidation, on the other hand, would look like lots of candles going sideways. When you think about these things, it's straightforward once you can visualise the logic behind them.

When we look internally for supply and demand areas, we are looking for areas that caused prices to move. So, in theory, on smaller timeframes, we would expect 'auction areas' before a significant drive. However, when you only assess one timeframe, what you see is usually within one candle.

Let me show you an example or two on the charts.

In this image, I want you to look at the string of green candles just left of the centre on the way up to the major swing high.

The range is shown in the following image.

This image shows the exact range I mean from the previous image.

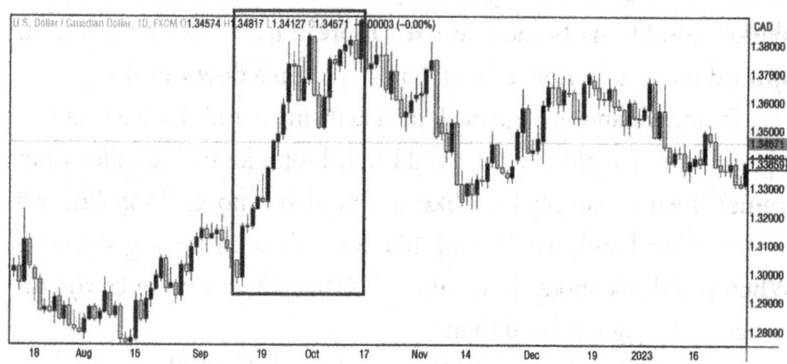

Now, I mark up the chart with a swing high and gaps like before, assuming we have not yet had the move down from the high.

I marked up the chart.

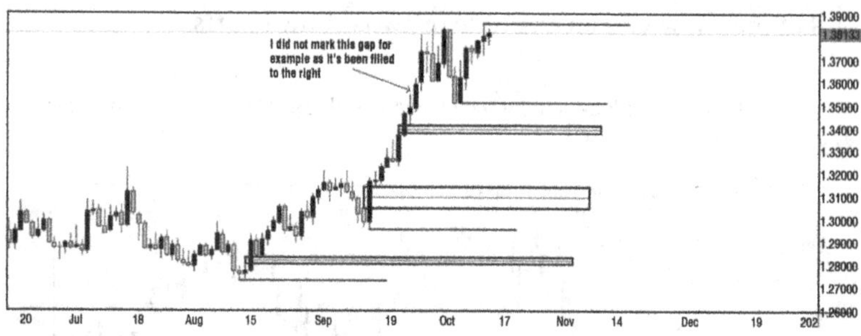

I didn't mark up every gap; just like in the example where the price was tagged, the gap was filled, but they would have been drawn until filled.

In *Master the Art of Trading* I talked about these areas being called 'Buy Before You Sell' and 'Sell Before You Buy' type moves. Some people call these order blocks. Regardless of what you call them, you only have to understand what is going on behind the scenes.

Let me highlight the area that fuelled the move up.

In this image, I have left the extreme high and low for reference and marked the 'power play'.

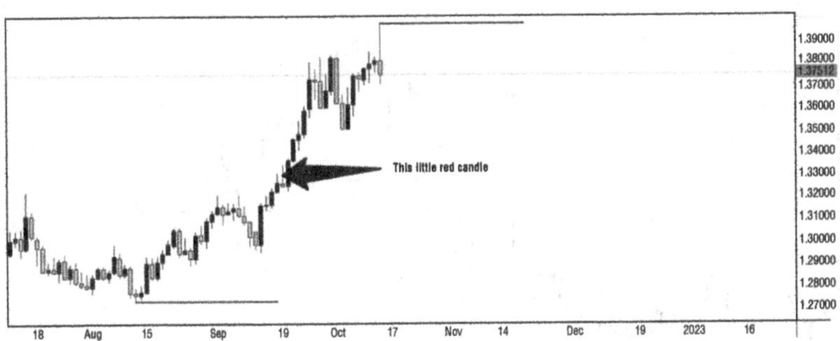

You see what happens after the little red indecision candle? It then had a significant green candle that caused a gap, suggesting a rally on the smaller timeframe charts.

Why did I say this caused a rally on the smaller timeframe charts? It can be seen here clearly, but in the shorter timeframe you would see a character change as the price broke above the old high from the move down. I will talk about bias in Chapter 21.

This area would be deemed as a significant demand zone. The reason is that sellers pushed the above price into this zone. Then, the price rallied significantly. This indicates a lot of buying here.

This image shows the same candle marked with a zone.

This image shows the price dropping back into that zone before moving up.

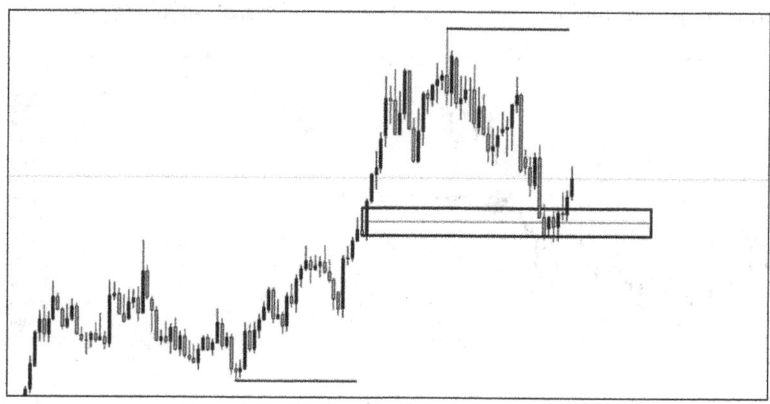

What this means is that we had sufficient demand here to allow the price to continue up.

This image shows the demand zone being used time and time again.

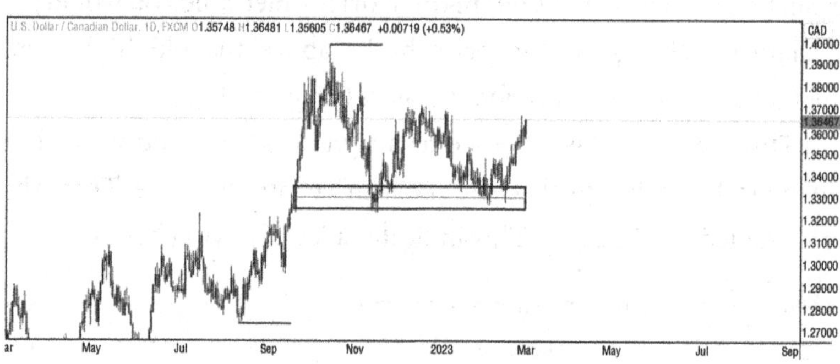

This is where many traders will see the price creating a support area. The price has tried and failed several times to penetrate this zone.

For supply zones, they are identical—only upside down. You are looking for a bullish indecision before an impulsive drop in price. Or, in other words, 'the cause'.

Much like everything else, this is not a silver bullet when it comes to trading. It's just another area to know and understand. These areas become magnets to price. The real value is when you start putting these techniques together, and you have a bias in terms of the general direction.

In this image, you can see the shorts of the Leveraged Funds are increasing.

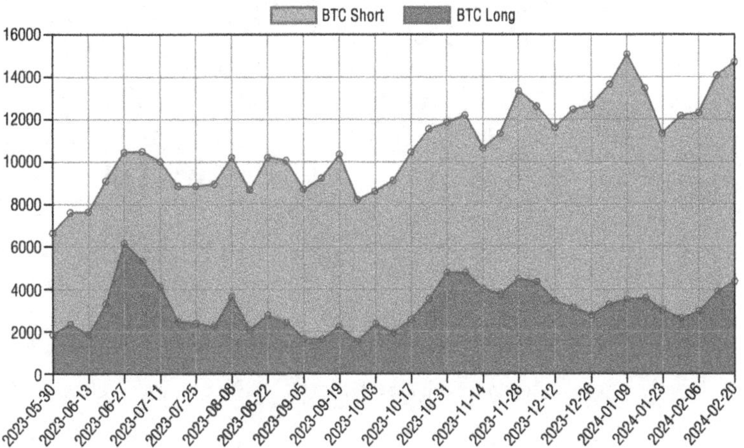

The situation today is very similar to that of the Gamestop saga a few years back, with retail traders' mentality of up only, diamond hands and memes on Twitter (now X.com).

It's scary to watch this play out in real time on such a large scale. You cannot warn them of the fate that awaits as, unless you post bullish sentiment that reinforces their beliefs, you are deemed stupid.

As they say, watch this space.

CHAPTER 20

COMMITMENT OF TRADERS

One of the main reasons I titled this book *Winning with Wall Street* is that these techniques allow you to be on the same winning side as the larger institutional players. The Commitment of Traders (COT) report is the closest thing you will find to understanding what Wall Street is thinking.

Just like the majority of indicators, this COT report is also lagging. You get data filed on Tuesday and released on Friday. So, in essence, it's a week old. You might say, what good is that?!

Now, think of the size of the institutional players; the positions they trade could take several weeks to accumulate or distribute. You see where I am going with this. . .

The COT publication is issued by the Commodity Futures Trading Commission (CFTC) in the United States. Again, you're not getting a full view of the industry, but you are getting a big enough sample size to help make informed decisions. The report provides a breakdown of the positions held by various market participants in the futures and options markets. The primary purpose of the COT report is to offer transparency into the activities of large traders.

Now, you might be licking your lips and thinking I have just given you the holy grail. Not quite. The data can be somewhat confusing; you wouldn't want to enter a trade based purely on this information.

In *Master the Art of Trading*, I covered this in depth. But actually, you don't need to extract a lot of information from it. When combined with the techniques I have written about here, you only need a glance at the COT data and you will see parts of the puzzle come together.

When trading assets such as commodities, there are a couple of key factors to put more emphasis on. For example, Open Interest is the total number of outstanding futures and options contracts for a particular commodity. Is this going up or down?

Then, you need to split this into each category or type of trader. I want you to think logically about this: if commercial traders are buying, non-commercial (speculators) are buying.

You now know the bigger traders are long, the speculators are professional traders not involved in the process or production, whilst the commercial traders will be involved in the production or in the chain somehow.

You will see a correlation, and ideally you want this to be in some kind of alignment.

Non-reportable positions, however, are the small traders or those whose positions are below the reporting threshold. These positions are aggregated into a single category.

Now, imagine you have these guys shorting into an area where the charts might suggest we have a key level. Retail will assume the level is likely to fuel a drop, whilst COT data suggests that the liquidity shows inflows of the big players buying this level up.

So, whilst it's not easy to break down, you might see a divergence between the speculators and commercials, for example. But this tool is only here to aid with your bias. Over time, you will get to notice patterns depending on the asset, the level and so on.

When it comes to forex and the S&P500, there is another category/report published by the CFTC. The participants are named slightly differently, but you have a similar situation.

When assessing something like Bitcoin or Aussie Dollar, for example, you would be looking mainly at the leveraged funds category. These guys typically include hedge funds and other large speculators that employ leverage in their trading strategies. Leveraged funds aim to maximise returns by using borrowed capital, often taking both long and short positions in various markets.

As you would classify these similarly to the speculators, they seek to profit from price movements rather than hedging against potential risks. They may have a higher risk tolerance and often engage in more aggressive trading strategies. So, they are really the ones to follow when trading shorter timeframes. I am still talking weekly and daily timeframes, not intraday.

You also have other tabs, such as dealers, other reportables and non-reportables. Much like the retail traders, these can be useful to know the sentiment in a general sense. You could find patterns yourself by comparing the divergence between the big boys and retail, for example.

Personally, I just simplify it. Does the leveraged funds situation fit with my chart bias? My Elliott Wave count: Do I see a slowdown in buying as we near a key level? This type of information is all I need.

Another player in this report is the asset managers. Note that these are very large in terms of the assets under management; their trade style is long, long-term. These are also institutional investors (e.g., pension funds, mutual funds and other managed investment funds). They are involved in managing portfolios of financial assets on behalf of their clients or investors.

Asset managers often use futures and options markets for hedging purposes or to adjust their overall portfolio exposure. Their trading strategies are typically more conservative compared to leveraged funds, focusing on long-term investment goals and risk management.

So, unless your strategy is a buy-and-hold for several years, this is also less important in terms of the info you want as a trader compared to being an investor.

There are traders who make complete strategies using COT data alone; there is nothing wrong with that. But when you add this to the overall directional bias, the larger Elliott Wave count and knowing your key levels, you can put yourself on the right side of the trade a lot more frequently.

CHAPTER 21

OBTAINING A BIAS

'In most bull markets there comes a time when the public controls fluctuations and the efforts of the largest operators are insufficient to check the rising tide.'

—Charles Dow

https://loveexpands.com/quotes/charles-dow-170052/

Obtaining a trading bias involves analysing market information and forming an opinion on the likely direction of an asset's price movements. This is where you can use your skills. For me, Elliott Wave is always the first go-to. I want to paint a roadmap. By this, I mean if I zoom out to a monthly timeframe. Then, I can get an existing count and see where we are. I'll check Fibonacci levels and get comfortable with the idea that it's more likely longer-term one way or the other.

Once I have my general bias, I can drop down to smaller timeframes. I might run some checks, like wave counts or fib levels. Then, if the bias is still the same, I will start adding clusters and gaps to the chart. I have found that on TradingView, I like to make monthly lines size 4, weekly size 3 and daily size 2. This gives me a visually pleasing view of the interesting positions at a glance on any timeframe.

Once you have this setup on the charts, you can look for the liquidity areas that match your bias. Again, test this on the charts.

If I review a chart like this, I can drill down to the smaller timeframes as I please. You don't need to count Elliott Waves on these smaller timeframes, as news-related events will influence them and can easily get invalidated. Elliott Waves are NOT the silver bullet.

For me, there are two schools of thought. First, retail is pure dumb money, given silly tools and looking at stupid timeframes, and then they add to that by looking at too many instruments while not deploying risk management correctly. Second, it's as simple as seeking liquidity, and retail always happens to be on the wrong side.

There are several other methods to obtain a bias, from zooming out and seeing if the chart is moving up or down.

Some people need a Moving Average (MA) for this: above an MA, it's up; below an MA, it's down.

One great yet simple way is knowing the liquidity pockets as a first requirement. So, draw them on your charts from monthly, weekly and down to daily. Then, go to the daily timeframe.

This shows critical levels in a monthly time frame.

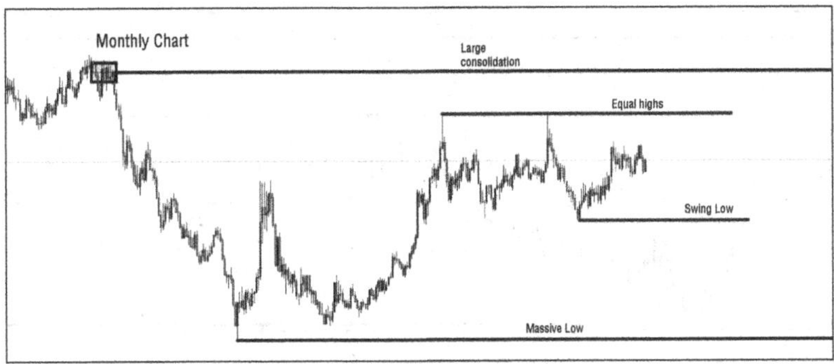

This only shows the primary monthly levels before I zoom in, using linewidth 4. If you want, you can also add consolidation and imbalance levels here. But for the sake of this example, it's more about showing the theory.

In this image, you can see I have added the weekly levels.

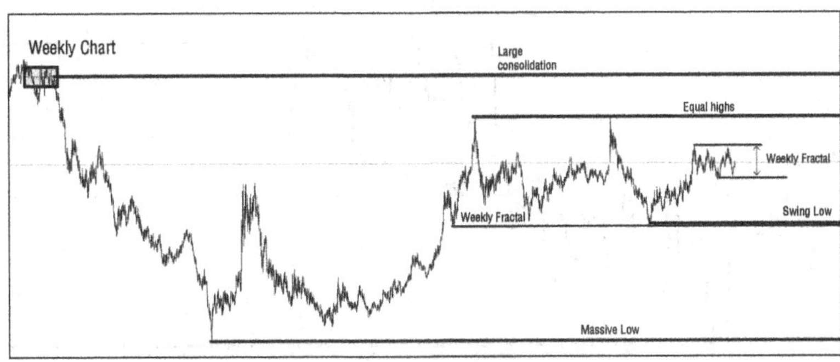

This level of marking up will take less than 2 minutes once you get into it.

This is now the same chart but zoomed in to the local swing up.

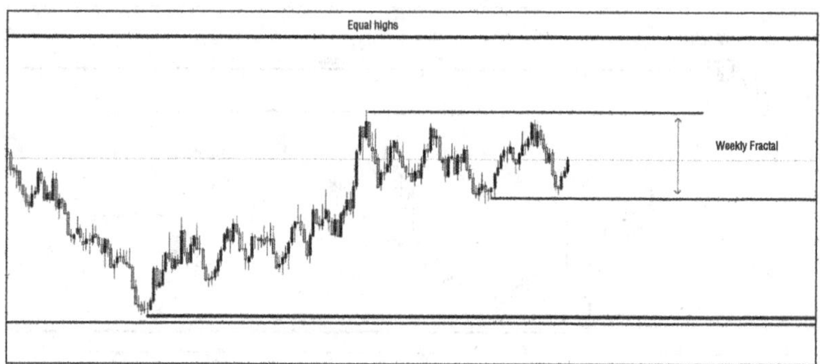

Once I am at this level, I like to add consolidation and imbalances. Now you know where on the chart I am looking, I will zoom in further for this example (a lot easier on the screen in front of me).

This shows the drilled-down levels.

In this example, you can see we have no weekly gaps. Only consolidation levels. The centre box has been tagged from above and rejected. This instantly could suggest a move back up to a higher level of liquidity.

We can repeat this on a daily timeframe.

Zoomed-in view, showing gaps that have been filled.

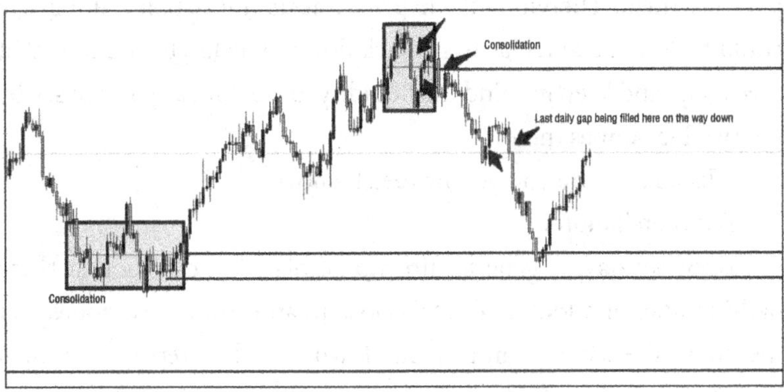

As you can see in this latest image, the gap fills as I write this. So, we can start looking for the swing from that low on the right up to the current price here.

You are drilling down and down and down to get a complete picture. Yet, none of this is all that technical.

You are showing the move from low to high with gaps left.

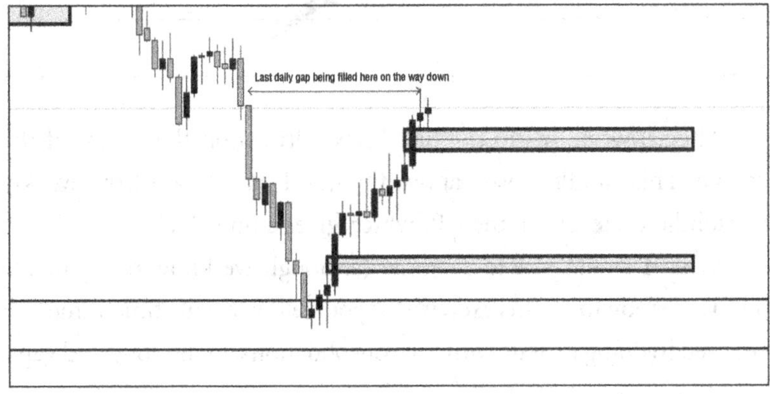

From this view, we can see two apparent gaps. The lower gap was partially filled. Therefore, if the price rejects this gap, it's filling. We could be looking at a bias to go back down. The target could be that lower gap, and keep in mind the liquidity just below, as you can see by the two black lines there.

Okay, I am sure you get the idea by now.

But there's more!

Now, we have a general directional bias. We can look at these daily candles and look at fractals close to and from these zones. Let me show the same example, but I will use bar replay to return from the low.

This shows from the low going up.

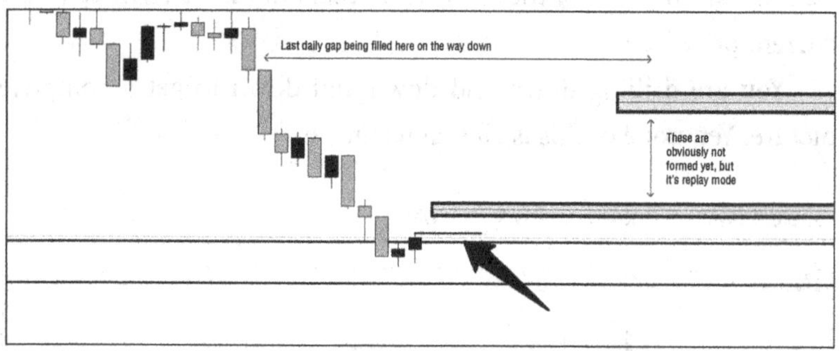

The arrow points to the line I have drawn on the height of the candle. This candle closed above the line I had drawn from weekly consolidation levels on the left, which gives a bullish clue.

What I would like to see now (although we know the outcome here) is for you to do this exercise for yourself on a daily timeframe and get used to doing it. Start with the consolidations, highs, lows and gaps.

The next candle is bullish.

This image shows a speeded up view of what's next.

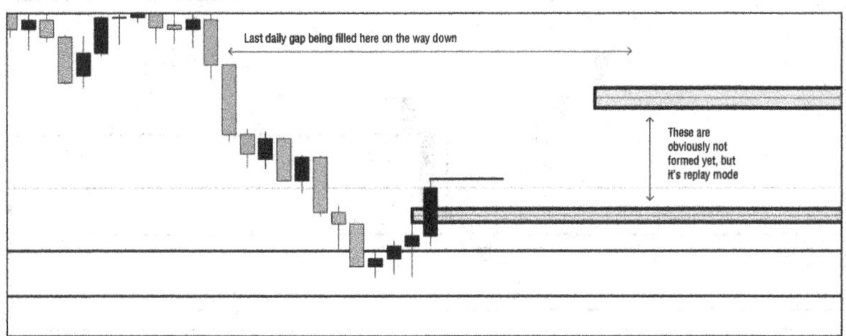

As we moved up, we have yet to see any change in the character. If you look left at this view, what is apparent is the gaps. The move up has cleared them. But as we are in bar-replay mode, they are obvious targets to work hand in hand with the bias.

This first red candle creates a gap.

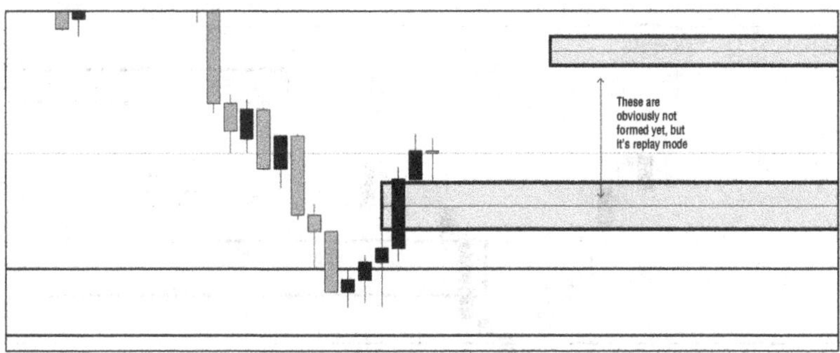

This could spell the end of the move; we would like to see how the next day fills the gap.

Showing what happens next.

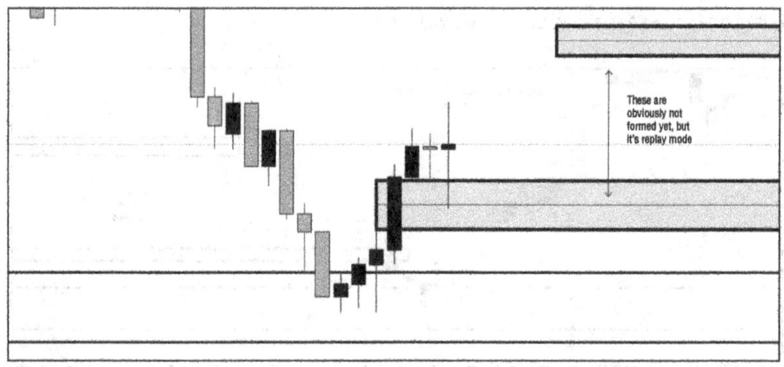

Look at this: it drops and fills 50% of that gap. But, in bias terms, we did not close red. It filled the gap and closed higher. This suggests the momentum is up, and this move into the gap was a pullback.

Showing the next couple of days.

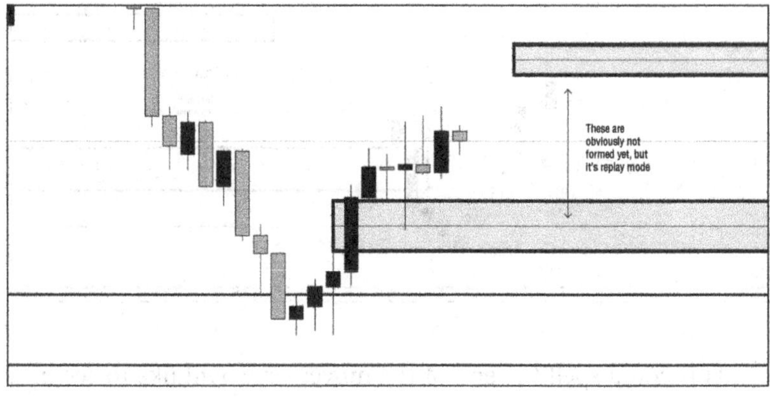

Nothing has changed. The momentum, although slow, would still suggest bullishness from the 50% gap fill. Let me explain why the next candle was red but did not close below the previous low. Then we get a solid bullish candle. The next red one is an inside bar that did not close below the lows. This would suggest momentum is still to the upside. Hence, my bias is still up.

If you are not following, read that again.

Now, this example is unfair; we know the outcome. But this works on the charts more than it doesn't. It would be best to define the close above or below the previous candles clearly. When you can be systematic, add your more considerable Elliott bias and the lines you drew on the higher timeframes.

Again, look how simple you can make it on yourself.

You can now look at a chart, and you are 75% plus positive you know where it's going, and you're probably 90% sure you understand why it's also going there. It's not a bad place to be when you're doing your technical analysis, is it?!

Showing a high and low level you are looking for.

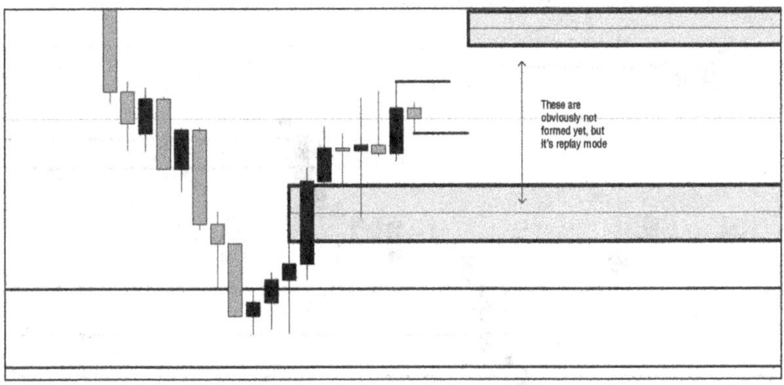

I have highlighted this here because the momentum to the downside would be a local low, although we could argue that an actual down move would not be in play until the candle low grabbed 50% of the gap.

This image shows a couple more candles and a break of the high range.

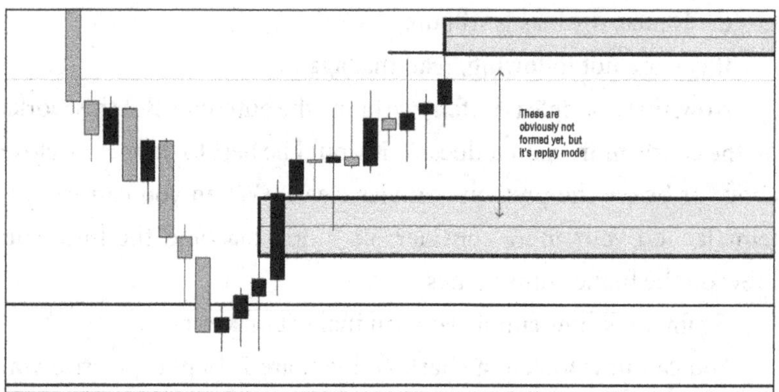

I jumped forward until we got the break-up. Not one candle there closed and changed the character. Which means the bias remains the same.

This image shows we broke again to the upside.

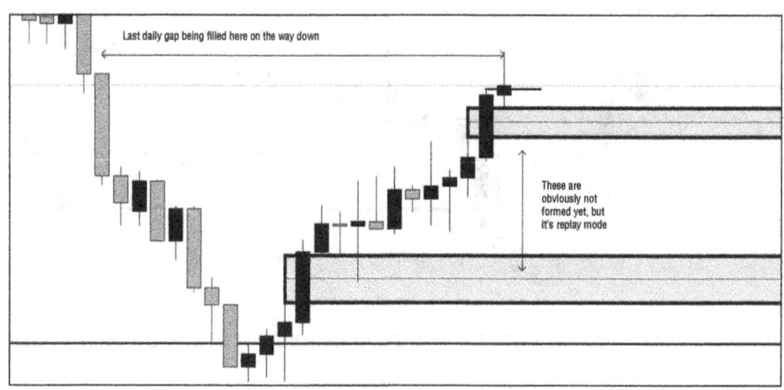

Not only did it break to the upside again, it created a gap. However, although we have a gap, we have no change in the character. This is bouncing from a critical level to the gap to the left. Does it mean the move has run out of steam?

Of course, at this stage, it is unclear as we still have upward momentum, but there is no character change yet. So, you would treat this cautiously.

This brings us up to today. So now we wait to confirm whether the weakness will drop or break through the gap. If it's down, we can look below at the gap levels. If it breaks above the gap over on the left, we can zoom back out and look for the next upside target.

I hope you can see how powerful this is. Especially when combined with the other techniques from earlier in this book.

Before we move to the next chapter, one parting thought is that the liquidity sequence is searching for the next pocket, which can be spotted from miles away. Just zoom out. Knowing which one it will reach for first is the real money maker. Practice this over and over again.

CHAPTER 22

VOLUME SECRET

'There is the plain fool, who does the wrong thing at all times everywhere, but there is the Wall Street fool, who thinks he must trade all the time.'

—Jesse Livermore

http://www.quoteswise.com/jesse-livermore-quotes.html

This chapter is about another useful trick in terms of obtaining a bias. Wouldn't it be nice to get more of a feel for why the price will go up or why it will go down next?

Well, this little secret will help with that for sure!

This technique is also valuable in any timeframe, but like everything else, the larger the timeframe, the more value or emphasis it should have.

This will seem obvious when you see it or when you test it. Let me start by explaining the difference between red and green candles. (It only really comes down to who's in control). In my previous book, *Master the Art of Trading*, I gave an example of each candle being like a sports match; it doesn't matter who spends more time in the opposition's half. The only score that counts is the final whistle. Where was the close? Up or down?

Having the insight will help assess the character and candle formations, especially at critical levels; this is also part of the story. The more you practice these techniques, the easier it will be for you to do without thinking. You will look at critical levels, obtaining your bias before starting your fundamental analysis. Much like driving a car, after a while, you nearly stop thinking about it; you just do it.

The technique will give you some clues to direction and general areas where the price will be attractive.

When you understand that the green candles indicate the final whistle that puts the buyers on the winner's podium, what does this mean for the bears, the seller and the losers in this candle?

They now have a choice—let the price run from them ('drawdown'), or they need to cover their position. By protecting that short position, they now buy. They are fuelling the price upwards.

So, start on a weekly timeframe (to practise this technique). Add a simple volume to the X-axis of the chart, like the image below.

In this image, you can see the volume on the X-axis.

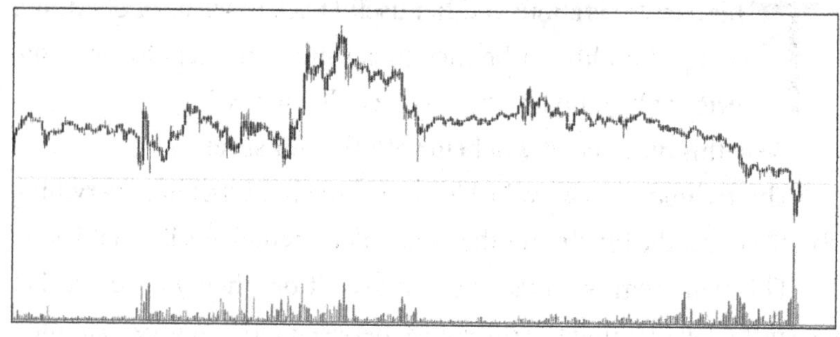

Now, on a more extensive timeframe (ideally monthly, weekly or daily), at least for the first couple of attempts at spotting these, what you need to do is look for large volume spikes. As you can see in the previous image (bottom right), the red volume is much larger than any other volume spike shown on the chart. It doesn't have to be this extreme, but I wanted to show it to be noticeable for the example.

Now, what I like to do is if the volume spike is red, I place a line from the bottom of the wick or the close of the body. This step is subjective, and you might find it works better for some pairs favouring one technique over other techniques.

This image shows the line I drew at the body close of the high-volume spike candle.

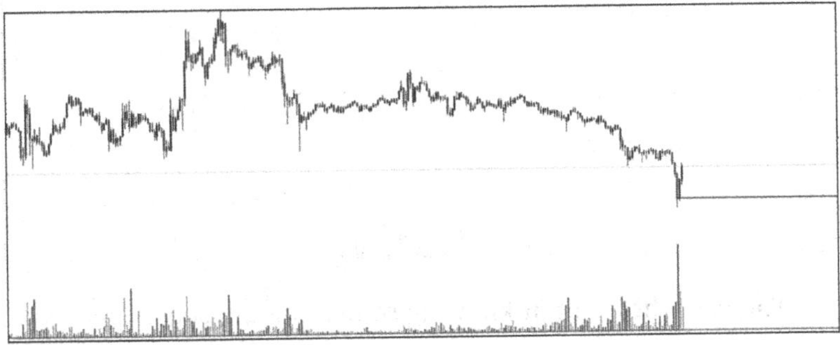

This becomes another 'interesting area', as traders are trapped on the other side of the move. Let's fast forward and see if you can visualise what this represents in the bigger picture. As in, what does it mean in logical terms? Why would this be interesting in the future?

This image shows that 66 candles later, we return precisely to this level.

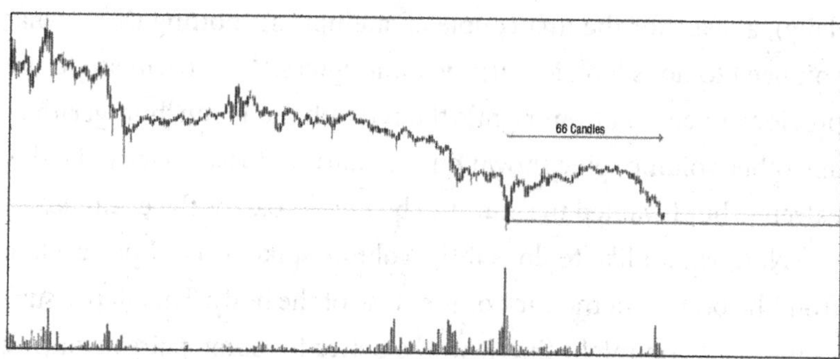

Was this an accident back to the exact level?

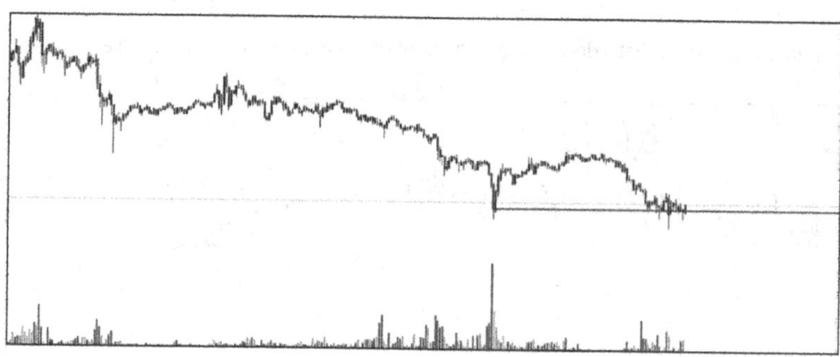

The value here lies in knowing something unusual happened at that volume spike. What sits under there? Liquidity, now the issue is—what type?

This image shows price-seeking long stops.

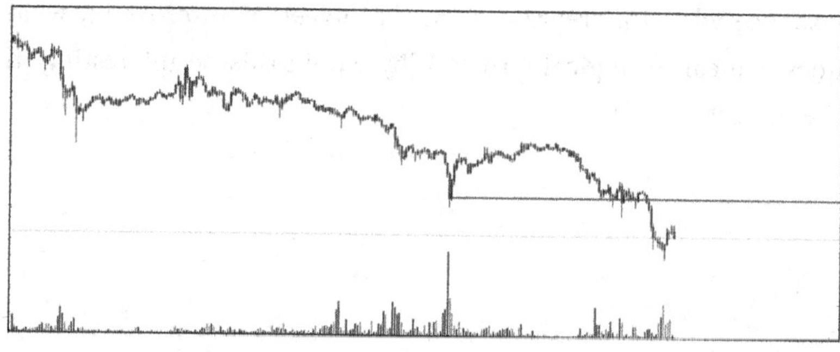

This is fuelling another move back up, as the subsequent apparent liquidity is up.

Jump forward.

Showing the price travelling up after collecting stops.

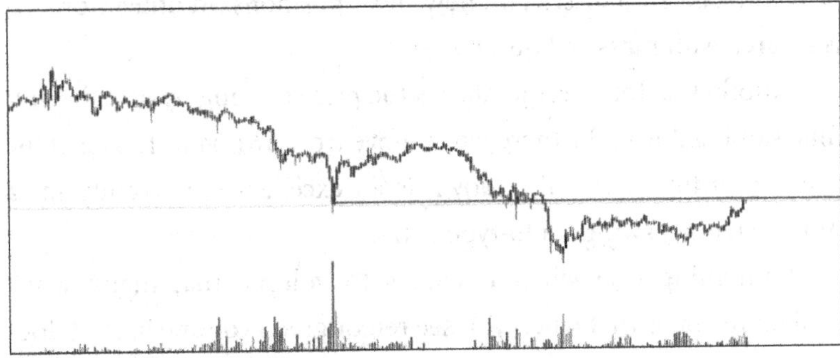

Next area of interest. Revisit the last chapter's concepts.

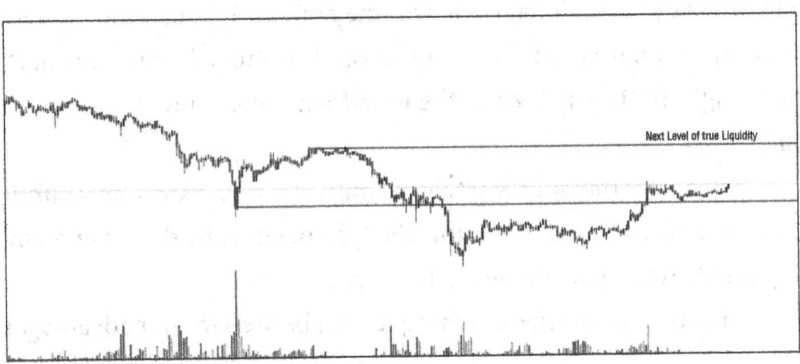

This image shows GBPJPY on a weekly timeframe.

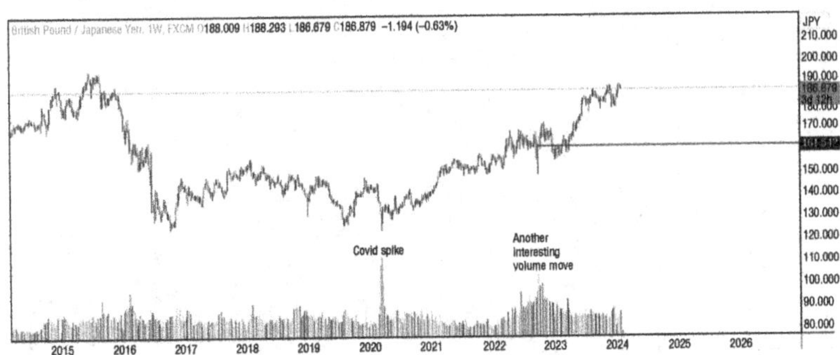

What this last image shows here is the COVID-19 spike standing out. Then, as we rallied up from that low, we had a sizeable green spike at the low. But as I said earlier, I placed a level at the high (due to it being green). This becomes a future level of interest, as there will be significant stop losses and new short positions. In other words, it is an area with massive liquidity.

Another factor to remember is the price moving up and the volume sloping down. So, there was a move from 161.54 to 186.82 at the time of writing. Returning down is an excellent opportunity for a more extended swing trade-type entry.

Something else when it comes to volume that many won't explain to you is that when you see red or green volume bars, it does not mean it was all buying or selling volume that actually took place. Let's say you look at the volume bar of a 1-hour candle. Now, let's say that bar is red. Then you drop down to a 15-minute chart; you might find that three of the four 15-minute candles were actually green.

Much like the sports pitch analogy, it's who won that counts. However, it's also useful to know the type of effort by the other team. Especially when you are near a key level.

Can you see how these techniques can be used to your advantage?

CHAPTER 23

CONFIRMATION

'A successful trader studies human nature and does the opposite of what the general public does.'

—William Delbert Gann

https://www.azquotes.com/quote/990256

Confirmation comes in many forms; the trick is knowing where you are looking for it to happen.

I have covered various techniques and where to spot areas of liquidity, but confirmation is the art of knowing what price is likely to do at a key area. You might have heard of terms such as Break of Structure (BoS, sometimes marked on a chart). Another term is Change of Character (ChoCh)—some people will attribute this to smart money concepts. But the reality is, it's a chart pattern that's been around forever.

Logically, in a trend, you are seeing both higher highs and higher lows.

This image shows an Elliott Wave count (0–5) illustrating higher highs and higher lows.

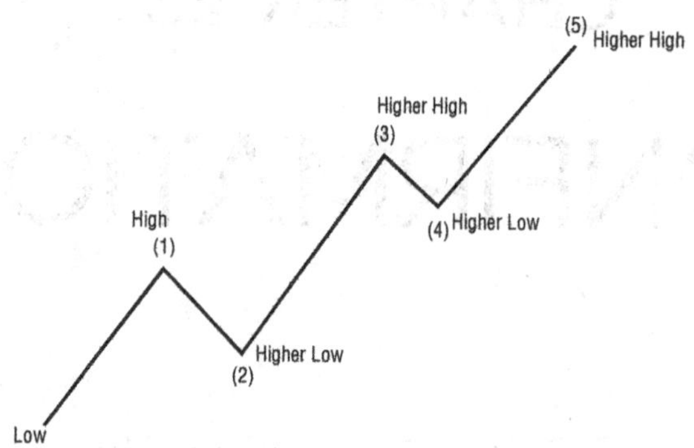

Naturally, in a downtrend, you will see lower lows and lower highs.

In the image above, you will see a break of structure as the price travels from 2 to 3. For example, this broke the structure high of 1 before completing a higher high at 3.

A change of character, on the other hand, is simply the chart spelling out that we have touched a zone of interest, taken liquidity and now changed direction.

If you imagine after an impulsive rally to the 5 high, let's say it reached an area of interest. You would now expect to see an A, B and C move down. So, let's look inside that move and show the change in the character.

This image shows a change in character.

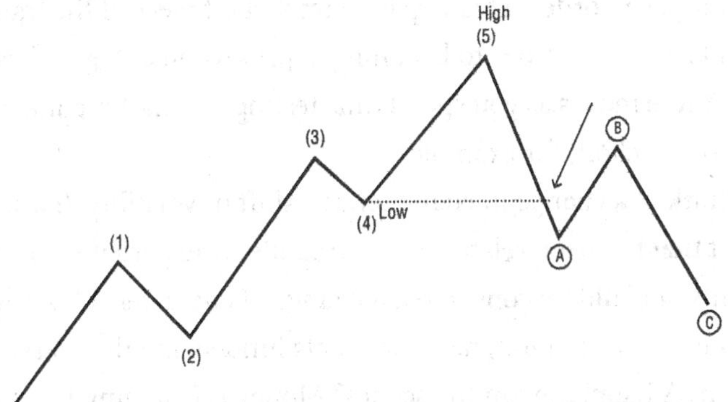

As the price travelled from the high 5 down to A, it broke the low of 4. This has changed the bias a little, as now we have a lower low.

It is not until B that we can also say we now have a lower high.

The actual change is not technically confirmed until making a new lower low under the low of the swing low A.

This image shows the confirmation of the change in character.

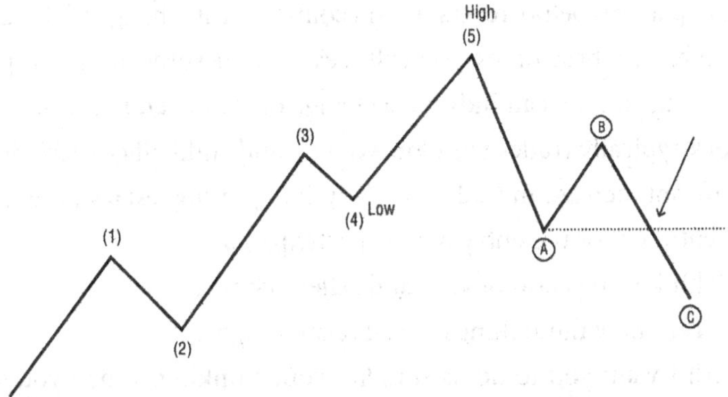

This is another topic I could write a full book on; however, for now, you get the general idea. You can combine this with key levels, Elliott extensions and, of course, liquidity areas.

Most traders don't wait for confirmation like this; they pick a level and set an order. This step is an important piece of the transition from playing as a trader to becoming a professional. You will start to notice these moves as you spend time testing the master pattern technique or Wyckoff, for example.

Think of a change in character as a shift in volatility. If a stock or market that has been relatively stable suddenly experiences increased volatility, it could be considered a change of character. This might be due to new information, news or events influencing the market.

What's happening in the scenes? Money is changing hands; buyers are exiting, for example.

When a trend is well-established (upward or downward), it's not going to be a swap at one price point; it's going to seek liquidity and play its little game to get buyers out and sellers in.

What I mean by this is that the move is likely to form a consolidation of sorts and then tag liquidity to tease retail into assuming the trend will continue. Then, a spike into liquidity regions (expansion of the master pattern) before reversing and confirming its change of character.

Often, at these times, you will see a volume surge; unusual spikes in trading volume can indicate a change of character. For example, if a stock typically trades with low volume and suddenly experiences a significant increase in trading activity, it might suggest a shift in market sentiment or the entry of new participants.

Think of Wyckoff buyers' and sellers' climaxes.

Crazy how these things are all related, right?

All I want you to do, is simplify your thinking. When you start your analysis now after reading this book, you will notice all of these things. The idea is to be able to see them play out in real time at a key area.

CHAPTER 24
JOURNALLING

'One emotionally-driven investment that causes massive losses is enough to keep you away from all investments for life.'

—Naved Abdali

https://www.goodreads.com/author/quotes/21662064.Naved_Abdali?page=3

You might think that this sounds obvious, even pointless. But you will not believe the power of keeping records of what you have done. This could include anything from the time and date of a setup through to what you were thinking to take this setup. Then, later, come back and add the outcome of the trade.

This information is priceless.

Journalling lets you analyse your trades. Looking back at your P&L to understand what you thought at setup and the outcome.

You will quickly realise patterns in both the winners and losers. (I could have put this under the psychology chapter, but it deserves a place on its own.)

I often find that when you tell someone to do this, they usually ignore it. But once you get someone who does it religiously, you see a vast improvement in their trading performance almost immediately.

This isn't just down to the fact that they noted their trade in a book and wrote an L (loss) or a W (win) later; it's knowing the time factor of entry, what day the entry was on, what pair and what the risk-to-reward ratio looked like. Then, of course, how it played out. Please include things like it took *x* hours to hit the take profit level, or I closed it early without hitting Take Profit as there was news due out.

Let's assume in 3 months you go through a bit of a rough patch, picking losers time after time. You can go through your journal and get a good idea of what has changed.

It doesn't have to be complicated. Like I said before, less is more—all too often, new traders come to me and say things like 'I want to make trading my profession' then ask questions like 'What do you think of this indicator?' Usually, this is on some small timeframe on a stock or coin nobody has ever heard of.

When you can show that the indicator didn't work seven times out of ten, or that news came out just after they entered a trade. It's a lot easier to spot and correct the issues.

You could use this technique to record win rates, risk-to-reward ratios; even tools or reasons for entry.

Over time, this will help you fix issues you don't even know are issues yet.

CHAPTER 25

DELTA (CVD)

'Do more of what works and less of what doesn't.'
—Steve Clark

https://onlinelibrary.wiley.com/doi/10.1002/9781119203469.ch9

This chapter, and the next, is not something you really need. But it does give you a good foundation so I decided to include both chapters more for your reference than as a suggestion to use either. Generally, the Delta tool is widely used with the footprint charts.

Volume Delta refers to changes or differences in trading volume; it may indicate the net difference between buying and selling volume at a particular price level or over a specific period.

When you combine the Delta with footprint charts, the general idea is to give you a deeper understanding. By this, you use the numbers inside each candle to calculate the momentum. I covered footprints earlier; if you remember, the buys and sells give the number of asks and bids inside the candle. The Delta is the mathematical equation of this data.

To understand the volume delta, you need to know that it's an indicator representing the net difference between buying and selling volume. In other words, it quantifies the aggressiveness of buyers and sellers in the market. This metric is handy in assessing market sentiment and identifying potential turning points. When the delta is aggressive one way over the other, especially after a long period in one direction, look at the examples in the previous chapters.

Can you see how you can include this in the same trading style?

The Delta is often presented as a histogram or line chart, showing the cumulative Delta over a specific period. A positive Delta indicates more buying volume, while a negative Delta suggests more selling volume. This can reveal hidden patterns and divergences, giving you a unique perspective on market dynamics.

So, footprint charts break down the market activity into smaller segments, typically price levels or clusters of trades. The Delta gives the cumulative picture.

Combining volume delta with footprint charts creates a powerful synergy; here's how these tools can complement each other.

1. *Identifying absorption and exhaustion.*

   By analysing the Delta at specific price levels on a footprint chart, traders can identify instances where opposing forces absorb buying or selling pressure.

   A positive Delta amid a downtrend may suggest buying interest or absorption of selling pressure, potentially signalling a reversal. Conversely, a negative Delta during an uptrend could indicate selling absorption and a possible reversal.

2. *Confirming trend strength.*

   Monitoring the volume Delta alongside footprint charts helps confirm the strength of a prevailing trend. A strong uptrend with positive Delta values reinforces bullish sentiment, while a downtrend with negative Delta values signals bearish solid momentum.

3. *Spotting divergences.*

   Divergences between price movements and volume Delta on footprint charts can be powerful signals. For example, if prices are making new highs, but the Delta is decreasing, it could indicate weakening buying interest, potentially foreshadowing a reversal.

4. *Analysing breakouts and breakdowns.*

   Volume Delta can provide valuable insights during breakouts or breakdowns. A surge in the positive Delta during a breakout may signify strong buying interest, supporting the sustainability of the upward move. Conversely, a negative Delta during a breakdown may indicate intense selling pressure, reinforcing the bearish trend.

5. *Understanding liquidity and order flow.*

   When combined with volume Delta, footprint charts offer a detailed view of liquidity at various price levels. Traders can observe where significant buying or selling activity is concentrated and use this information to assess potential entry and exit points.

6. *Fine-tuning entries and exits.*

   Combined volume Delta and footprint charts allow traders to fine-tune their entries and exits. For example, a trader might look for a positive Delta and intense buying activity on the bid side before entering a long position, seeking confirmation of a supportive market environment.

7. *Dynamic risk management.*

   Volume Delta can aid in dynamic risk management. If, during a trade, the volume Delta starts to show signs of divergence or weakening trend support, a trader might consider adjusting their stop-loss levels or exiting the position.

One recent example I have used is the current delta view on Bitcoin.

The Delta showed positive momentum from $1 up to the first real all-time high at $65,000. But then it flipped red. So, although we rallied up to $69,000, it was running on fumes.

This shows the flip in the Bitcoin momentum.

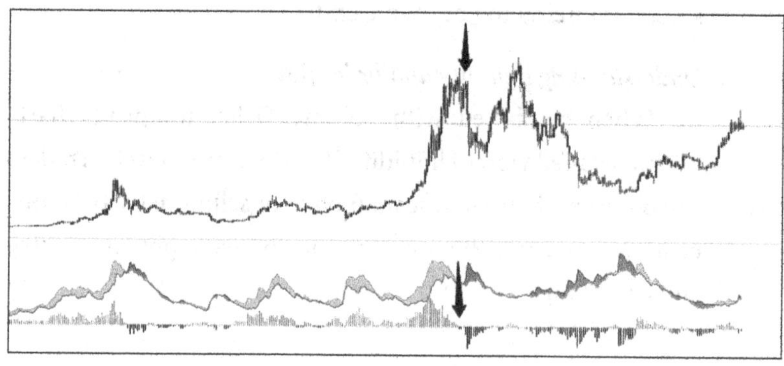

The suggestion of such a move back up and above the old all-time high at $65,000 was the market seeking liquidity from all the sellers at the top in terms of stop losses and, of course, new buy orders at $65,000 or greater. It was fuelling the drop.

I shared a post on the way to the $69,000 (https://www.tradingview.com/x/uwJUDZ6M). I explained why we would see a move just above $65,000 and a fast drop back down. After reading the last 24 chapters, I hope you can see the logic was already pre-programmed.

Here's the image.

This image shows the call as to why we would fall and rise, then drop hard.

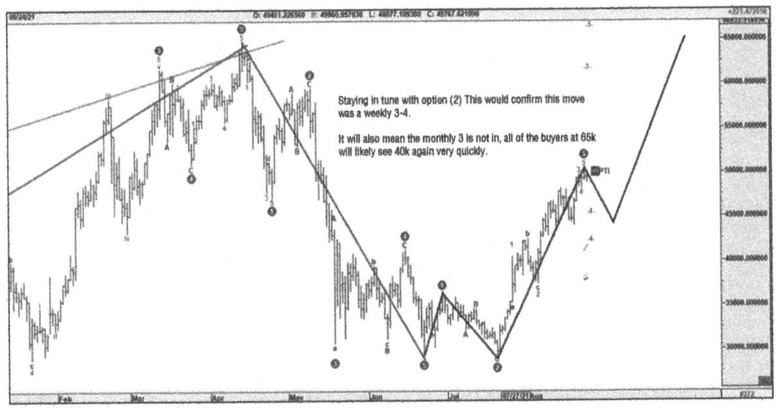

Well, it's no surprise it dropped as I expected. It rose to just above that first major all-time high of $65,000, and it dropped to $45,000. Where it then created a re-distribution and fell to a $15,000 region. So how could I foresee this in August for a move that didn't complete until November, and the drop-down bottomed the following November?

Liquidity combined with a predisposition and the wealth of knowledge you've just acquired.

CHAPTER 26

DELTA CVD WAVES

One other thing worth mentioning here is the Delta Waves. I don't use them, but let me give you an example and explain them—I think this will help you understand the logic of these moves.

Let's go back to what I said about the cumulative Delta and visualise the buys and sells (think Wyckoff) when observing the cumulative Delta values over time. To understand the concept, let's break down how buying and selling activities in the market contribute to forming these patterns.

Step by step.

1. Cumulative Volume Delta (CVD)

   Definition: Cumulative delta is a measure that represents the net difference between buying and selling volume at each price level over a specified period.

Calculation: It is calculated by summing the Delta values at each price level as market orders are executed.

Interpretation: A positive cumulative Delta indicates more buying volume, while a negative Delta suggests more selling volume.

2. Zig Zags

Definition: Zig zags in the context of trading charts refer to patterns of alternating upward and downward movements.

Formation: Zig zags are created by the continuous oscillation between bullish and bearish sentiment in the market.

3. How Buys and Sells Create Zig Zags in Cumulative Delta

Accumulation of buys: In a bullish zig zag, there is a series of aggressive buying activities. Traders are placing market orders, leading to positive Delta values.

Cumulative delta rises: As buying volume exceeds selling volume, the cumulative Delta rises, indicating a positive net difference.

Upward movement: This positive cumulative Delta contributes to the upward movement in the price.

Now, think about the bearish aspect of this.

Accumulation of sells (not to be confused with distribution): In a bearish zig zag, there is a series of aggressive selling activities. People are executing market orders to sell, leading to negative Delta values.

Cumulative Delta falls: As selling volume exceeds buying volume, the cumulative Delta decreases, indicating a negative net difference.

Downward movement: This negative cumulative Delta contributes to the downward movement in the price.

4. Market Dynamics Driving Cumulative Delta Zig Zags

   Shift in sentiment: Zig zags often occur due to shifts in market sentiment. People react to news events, economic indicators or technical patterns, leading to buying and selling pressure changes.

   Reversals and corrections: Cumulative Delta zig zags are particularly relevant in trend reversals and corrections. A bullish zig zag might indicate a potential upward reversal, while a bearish zig zag may signal a possible downward reversal.

5. Analysing Cumulative Delta Zig Zags

   Confirmation of trend: Traders use cumulative Delta zig zags to confirm the strength or weakness of a prevailing trend. For example, a bullish zig zag during an uptrend may signify continued bullish strength.

   Market conditions: Different market conditions may influence the significance of cumulative Delta zig zags.

   Understanding the ebb and flow of buying and selling activities in the market is a handy skill. This can gain insights into potential trend reversals, confirm existing trends and identify critical support and resistance levels.

For me, all of this could fit into a simple paragraph. Knowing if buying or selling is increasing is enough. Combine that with critical levels you have identified with your bias, and you don't need much other than good risk management.

I wanted to include both the Delta information and the zig-zag concept to fill the book with more words. No, I'm only joking. The idea was to help you visualise the concepts.

These zig zags can give clues in terms of momentum. The CVD oscillator also offers similar types of clues. But I will say what I said earlier: less is more if you think of it in simple terms. Instead of having nasty shocks, the price is flying through a consolidation zone or gap; if you grasp what buying and selling under the hood looks like, you are one step ahead of other retail traders.

Combine this with your Elliott Wave directional bias. It is as simple as knowing the levels.

I've been in this space a long, long time, and I often see the same issues with new traders. The more you dig, the more complex you make it for yourself; you end up confusing the matter, and you will become nervous if everything doesn't align.

So don't put yourself in that situation.

CHAPTER 27

PUTTING IT TOGETHER

'If your goal is to trade like a professional and be a consistent winner, then you must start from the premise that the solutions are in your mind and not in the market.'

—Mark Douglas

https://www.goodreads.com/author/quotes/148119.Mark_Douglas

As I said right at the start, this book was all about getting you to think and act like a professional trader. People assume you need courses and indicators to get to this level. The truth is, as I hope I have demonstrated here in this book, you can obtain enough information from a naked chart and a little understanding.

While volume tools and footprint candles look fantastic on a screen, they can easily cloud your judgement. Knowing the information written in the charts is what will allow you to make informed decisions with a systematic approach. Trading is all about statistics; if you use a 5:1 risk-to-reward ratio, you can practically be wrong more than you are right and yet still make money.

What I have covered here should allow you to find not only 5:1 or greater setups but, in addition, you should be right a lot more now than you are wrong because you understand the logic.

As a final recap, I will try to simplify this enough for you to have almost trigger points. You can always go back and read through the book again. But I ask you to try these techniques on a demo account in bar-replay mode. Get a good understanding before risking capital.

The number one starting point. . . risk management.

As I just said, the statistics will always be on your side if you have good risk management.

The next step, pick one or two instruments and learn the best you can. Think of these like learning a language; the more you try simultaneously, the less of an expert you become in one. Some gold traders look at nothing other than gold; the same goes for oil and many other instruments. There are always opportunities, even when only using one chart.

Then, zoom out.

Get that bias nailed down, and see the wood through the trees. Spot all the apparent levels and get a rough idea of your Elliott Wave structure. Don't marry the idea, but you should spot the obvious on these timeframes, monthly and weekly. If you can't, don't worry; this is where you may flip to another instrument. Maybe spend more time on a demo account, go back decades and apply an Elliott Wave count up to the current price action or the local swing high or low.

On a monthly timeframe, it could be several years back to its local swing high or low.

Once you have the general bias, focus on areas of interest and find gaps and consolidations. Mark them up and try linewidth sizes and colours you can quickly identify. Go from your monthly view down to weekly, and repeat the process. Then, drop once more to the daily.

Before you jump into a trade, try a couple of tests—do some backtesting, spend the first couple of weeks, even months, testing instruments and don't get upset if you get good on one you hadn't intended on trading. Most of my students since 2020 have been crypto fanatics. I would say at least 30% lean more towards trading forex over crypto since being educated.

Once you get your charts marked up, you have tested them and are happy, try a month or two on a demo account. This is a skill for the rest of your life. Think like this, and you will do alright.

Here's a walkthrough example.

Zoomed right out.

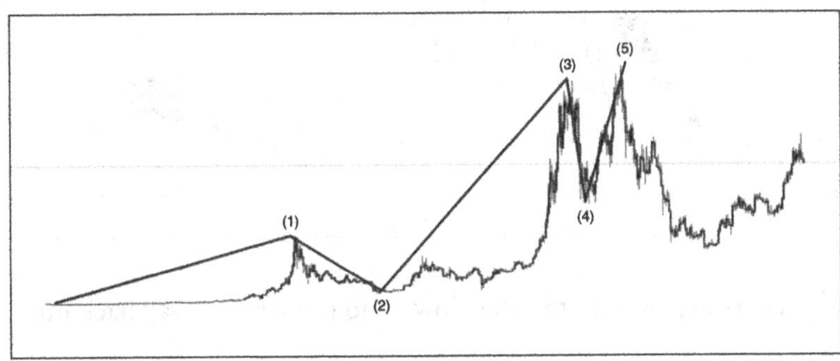

Clear Elliott Wave counts 1–5 are visible here. Now, we are looking for a corrective move.

This image shows a prominent area of interest in a cluster where prices are consolidated.

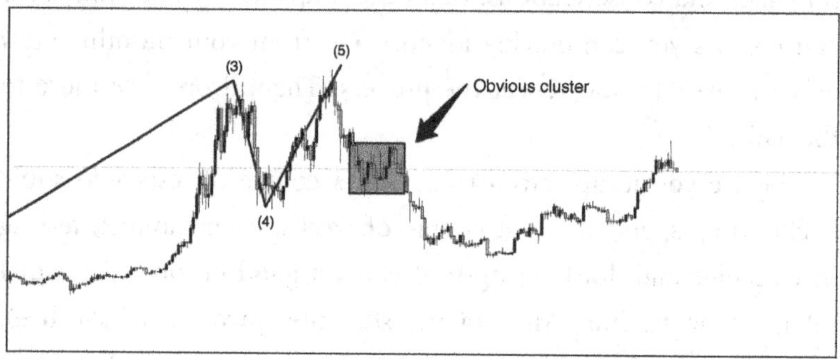

Does the move below 1 look as impulsive as the previous sudden wave X?

This image shows the lack of motive momentum—a great candidate for a B move rather than an impulsive up move.

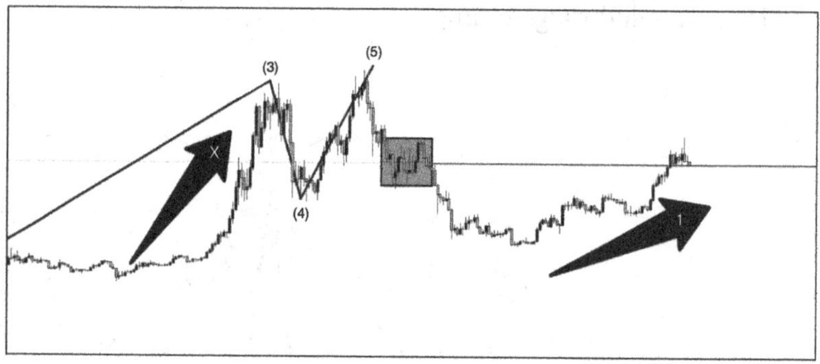

There are gaps on the way down and gaps on the way back up.

This image shows all the gaps from high to low and low to the current price.

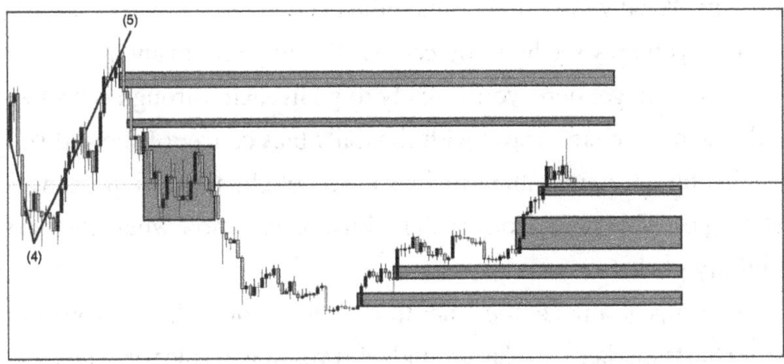

As you can imagine, we have grabbed liquidity to the upside by returning to the consolidation range. We are likely 5 top, A down and B back up in Elliott Wave terms.

You can start to paint the big picture with a couple of simple steps. Based on this last image, where would you guess the most liquidity is sitting?

This image shows the volume profile with a box around it.

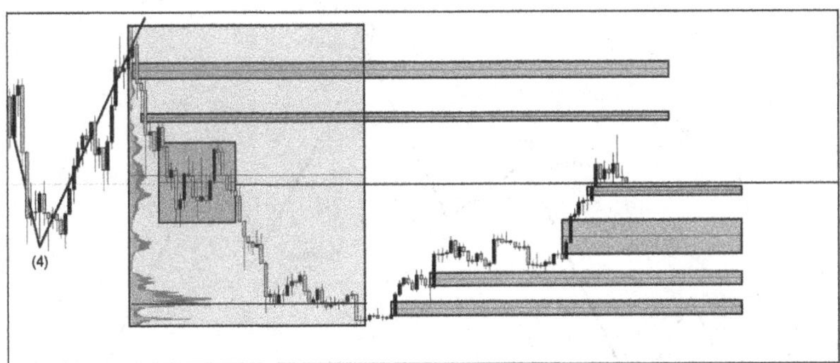

Price created a move from high to low, or 5 to A. The point of control is down low, and then the price moves up, grinding to the next significant level it created on the way down. On its way there, it left gaps. What would these gaps indicate?

Can you now see how you can use this to your advantage?

Once you get here, you're ready to go live. Go through each step and watch the charts travel with the daily bias concept I showed you in Chapter 21. Remember, the bias does not change until it changes (stating the obvious!). Don't rush in. Ensure you know where the next liquidity pocket is.

In terms of some of the other things I have covered, once you have your charts marked up, play around with volume profiles or even footprints and Delta. What you will see is where you have your lines and zones. You will see the same levels you identified without needing them.

For the final check, take a glance at the COT report. Before you know it, you will be on the right side of the trade more often.

You can then remove them and keep clear charts and a clear mind.

Revert to statistics—risk management is critical; a 3:1 reward-to-risk ratio or greater will make your job so much easier in the long run!

Here are a few charts to show you the concept overlapping.

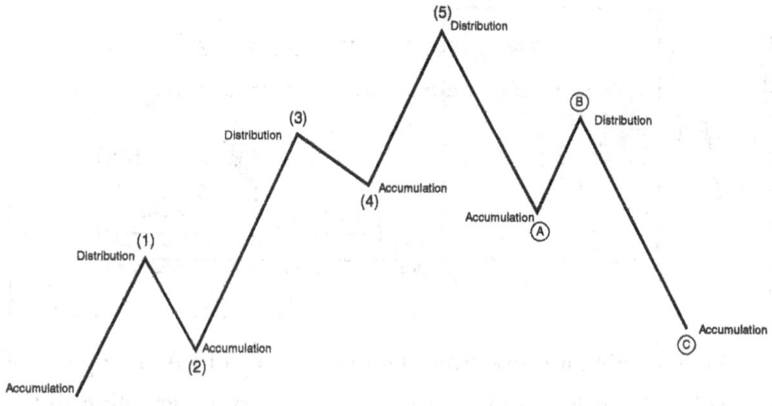

In the previous image, you will notice on smaller timeframes the areas of accumulation and distribution. I market these as an example of where you would expect them from an Elliott Wave perspective.

Now, if you take a look at this next image, I have used the same chart and marked lines in terms of price points around liquidity.

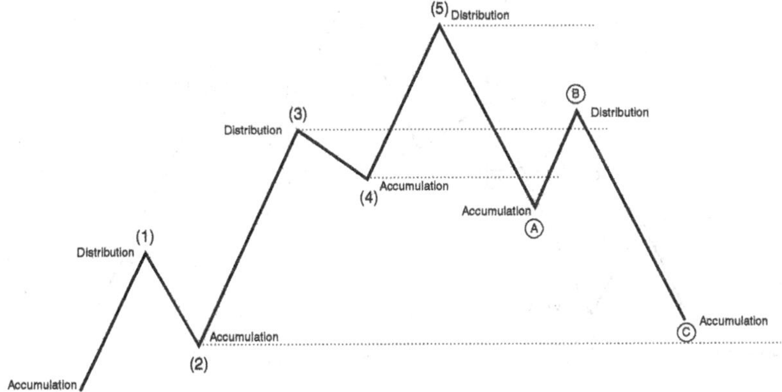

You might not see how obvious this is. I encourage you to do some testing on this, and you will quickly notice the patterns.

If you can imagine a horizontal line from 2, there will be liquidity under this as it's filled with strong buyers. So, as the price rallied up to 3 and then pulled back to form 4, the price left internal liquidity pockets. As the price rallied from 4, breaking the old high 3, it accelerated to a new high 5 before dropping, leaving external liquidity above 5. The magnetic pull on price will be back to the levels (3 and 4) before moving from A to B to make retail traders think we might want to go back up. This is why these levels often overlap. The obvious target is the run to the lower-level liquidity left all the way down at 2—of course, this won't always be as textbook.

If you were to zoom in several timeframes, you would see minor waves inside the waves, and these would create imbalances and master pattern-type clusters. But all you are seeing is a move to the bigger cycle's run to liquidity.

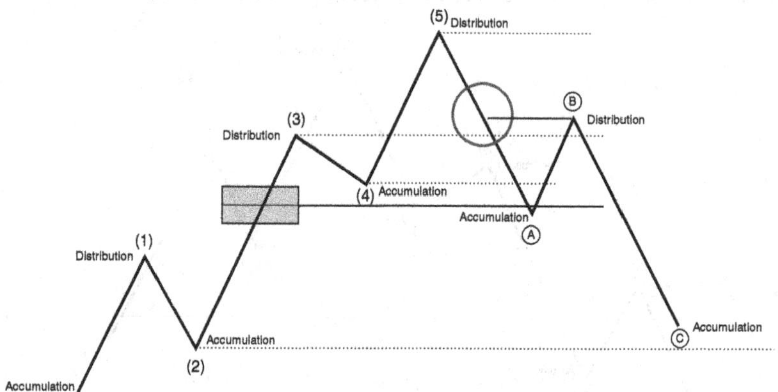

In the image above, you will likely see some master pattern of the smaller (3 to 4) inside the larger (2 to 3) move shown in the chart. On the right, the drop from 5 to A might be aggressive and probably left some kind of imbalance.

Although these are textbook examples and won't always play out like this, you will start to find similar results in similar locations quite frequently.

In this image you can see the highest level of liquidity.

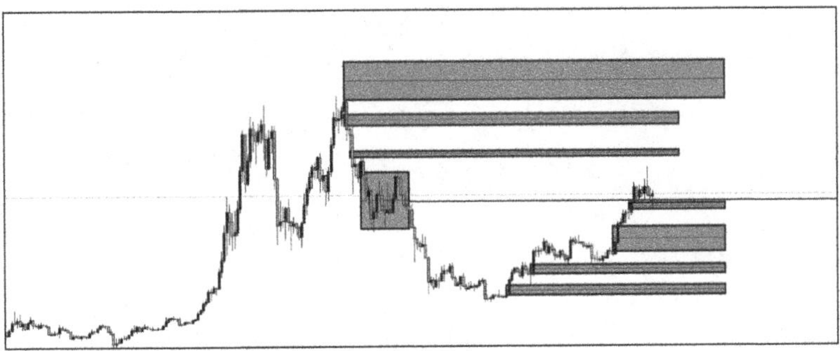

You can clearly see the areas of interest. The large box at the top would obviously represent new buyers above the current all-time high. However, in addition it will likely have a lot of selling pressure there also.

CHAPTER 28

EXECUTING A TRADE

'The world's greatest traders have all walked the exact same path you are on right now.'

—Nial Fuller

https://za.pinterest.com/stephandrep/trading-quotes/

I guess executing a trade is what many people fail to bring together. You have just read through a pile of practical information written in hindsight. Now what?!

First, you must remember that not all charts will be textbook. All you need is a little common sense and a splash of logic.

If you go through the last chapter, you would start from a big picture view, out on the monthly or weekly, for example. First things first. Obtain your overall trend direction.

This image shows a weekly chart of USD JPY as of 27 February 2024.

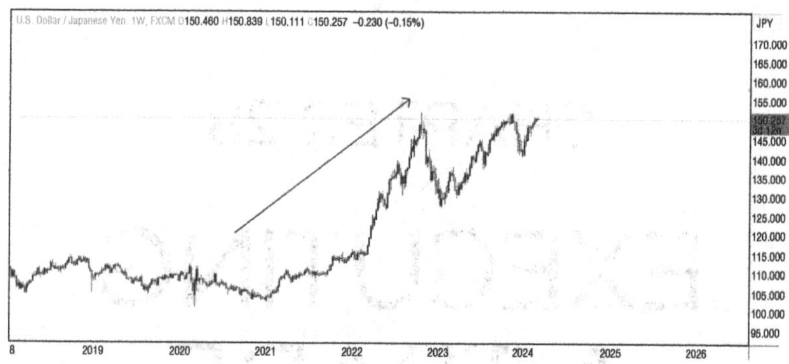

I would safely say the chart shows a large uptrend in the general sense.

In this image, I have drawn liquidity lines, both external and internal.

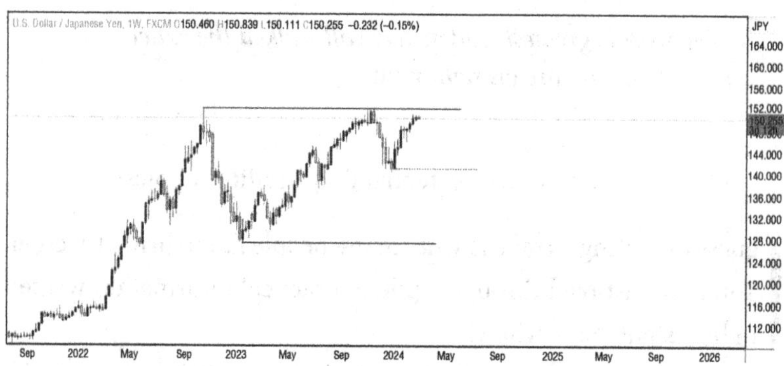

Now, if I drop down to a daily timeframe, what am I looking for next?

I have used a daily chart in this image and added internal liquidity levels along with two obvious gaps.

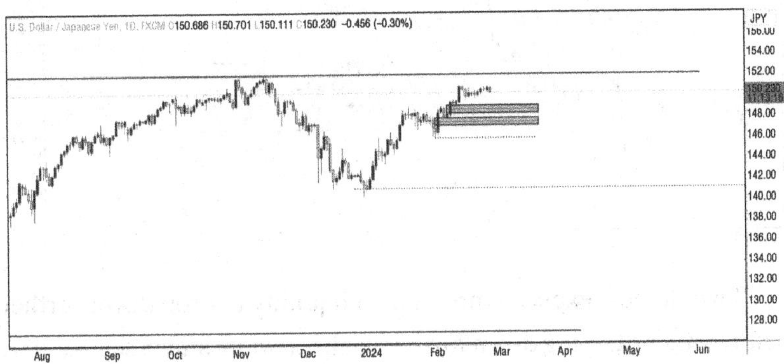

This image shows the 4-hour equal highs, the weekly external and daily internal levels, along with the gaps.

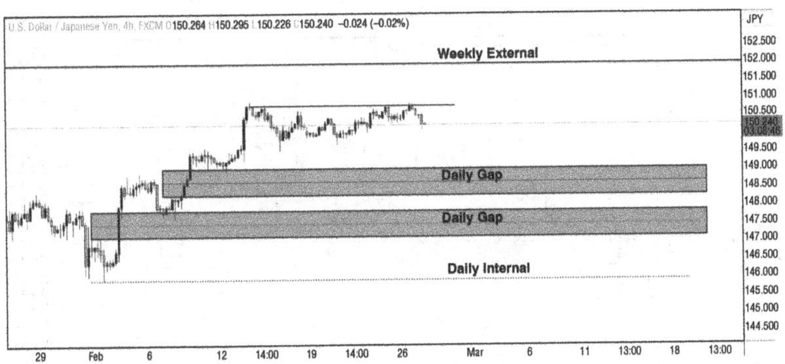

Without talking about Wyckoff or Elliott Wave Theory I could add these, but in the simplest form I now have a pretty good view to operate from.

In this image, you can see the price is squeezing up, making higher lows but losing upward momentum.

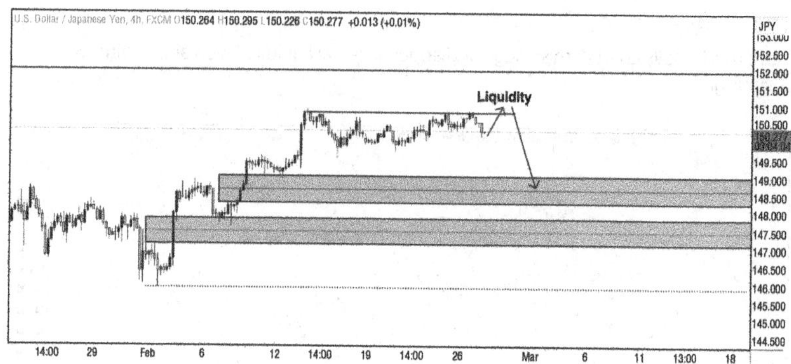

I would now expect a move up on liquidity to drop down further before either carrying down further again or going after a second dart up for the weekly external level above, near the 152 price point.

In this image I have marked up an entry at the arrow; just above the liquidity line on a 4-hour with an SL at the weekly external point and a TP into the gap of the daily below.

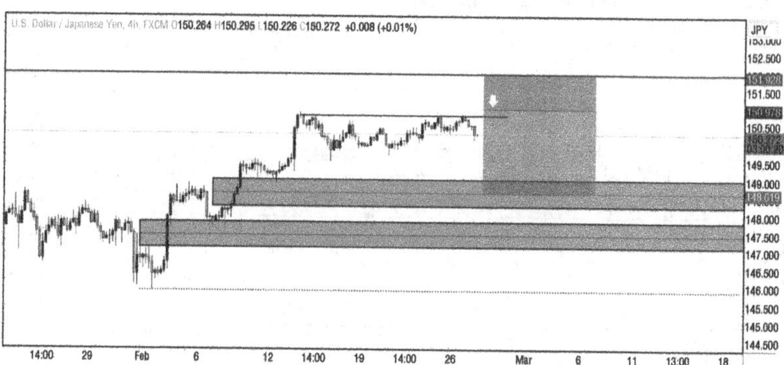

This is only one example scenario. I wouldn't just set an order and wait for a touch; I would assess its character if we were near the level. Trading is all about being reactive to price and not trying to predict its exact levels.

Next, we could do this another way. Follow the same steps but now, can we see from a daily candle where the draw on liquidity is likely to be and why?

In this image, you will see the previous day's highs and lows marked up.

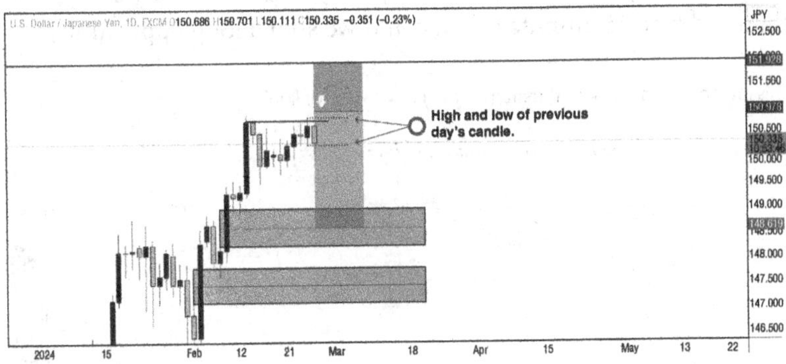

If you recall what I showed in Chapter 21, you can clearly see we have tried to drive down below and currently back above. This would suggest the draw on liquidity down has occurred today and will likely target back above. Think of the market sequence chasing liquidity.

So, the inverse is the second way you could attempt to trade this. We assume we need to move up to grab liquidity to come down harder. So, what about a long entry on a smaller timeframe?

Again, I have chosen to ignore Wyckoff and Elliott Wave Theory here. To show how you could break it down even in simple form, adding an Elliott bias is only going to increase your chances. Let's assume we know it's in distribution (a good sign, seeing it slow as we near a weekly level above after a strong uptrend).

Let's say we are at an Elliott weekly 1, 3 or 5 for the sake of this example. We are seeing a slow in the price action. We are at a critical level; roughly 152 would be outside liquidity. You see how I built a pretty compelling bias already.

If the market is wanting to come down, why would you go long?

Well, now that's a timeframe thing. This is precisely how you can use this book to your advantage. Let's assume I see this going short after grabbing liquidity; I still think it's on the 4-hour timeframe and viewed out on the daily timeframe. If we drop down to, say, a 1-hour followed by a 15-minute chart, could we spot a long opportunity?

This image shows a 1-hour timeframe and a low sweep of liquidity.

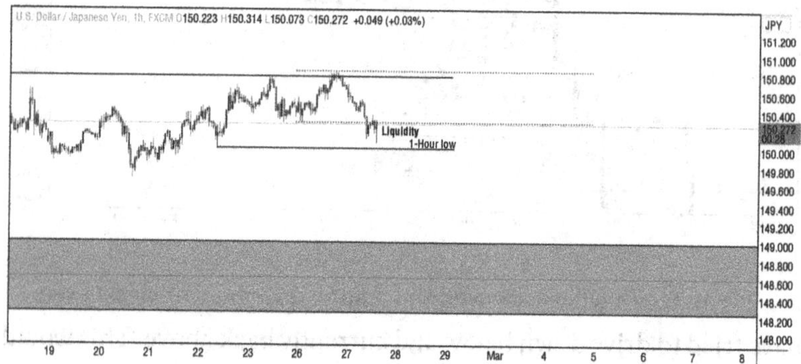

We have created equal highs above, we have swept liquidity below; there is a pretty good setup (providing the risk-to-reward ratio is also in our favour to make a long trade). Something like this.

The image shows where you 'could' set up a long entry.

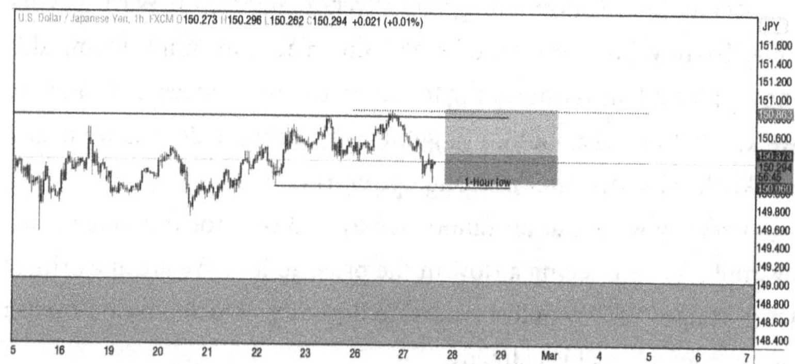

The only issue here is that the stop loss is below the recent low and the take profit, being just above the high, means the risk-to-reward ratio is only 1:1.6. Which is not ideal.

So, why didn't I show you a textbook example?

Well, just like trading, they don't always line up as you would like. Although we could probably take this trade with many factors in our favour, if we don't stick to a 2:1-type setup or greater, then we can easily change the statistics to not be favourable to our long-term goals.

Just as I mentioned at the end of Chapter 18 relating to the current Bitcoin price, the issue is simply risk to reward. If you bought at $50,000 and now expect it to travel to $100,000, where is your stop loss?

If you bought it sub $1000 then it's a different game.

Regardless of the asset or the instrument, when placing a trade risk to reward is crucial. Unfortunately, many newer traders learn this the hard way or actually don't learn it even then, they simply blow their accounts.

I know many of you would have either already traded Bitcoin or read books like this to learn about Bitcoin. Trade execution is key, especially with something as volatile as Bitcoin. Here's a recent example of why I wouldn't be interested to buy, even knowing the price was moving up.

I have to aknowledge my average entry was just above $200, so entries at $15,000, $20,000 or $30,000 made no sense to me personally. In addition to this, I publicly posted three options from the $15,000 low in November 2022.

The first (best) option for the bigger picture was a slow accumulation. This option was actually published in my previous book.

The second (okay) option was that price had not actually come into accumulation yet and there was still a much bigger corrective move from the $69,000 top in November 2021.

The third (worst case) option was that we would likely see a triple top move, meaning from $15,000 to roughly the $60,000–$70,000 region before another correction would take place.

This image shows option one (published in *Master the Art of Trading*).

This image shows the post talking about option two having its corrective A to B move.

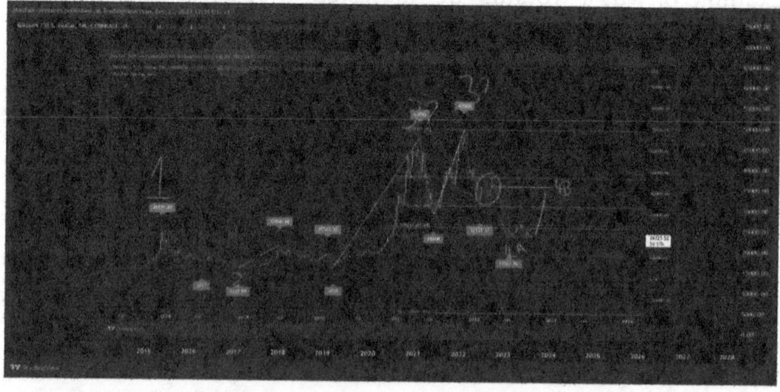

This shows the triple top option three.

I included this here as it's the perfect example of risk to reward.

When you think of the psychology behind such moves, I want you to note why I painted three scenarios. I am working with the chart and not trying to predict it.

The Elliott Wave count had a potential large scale 1 at the $69,000; the move down to $15,000 could be 2 or A, hence option one being the zero for an impulsive move up.

If it was only A at the $15,000, then you would expect a long B—think about liquidity and how many new entries the price would attract in this asset with its hype.

Option three meant that if we were impulsive, we would work the Fibonacci levels from the low, giving estimated targets around the $65,000–$75,000 region.

Now, if you bought at $200, where is the confirmation or need to buy more at the break of the accumulation zone? Remember, B might have only seen us go to the $50,000–$53,000 range. The risk would, therefore, be a stop loss under $15,000, entry at roughly $33,000 and a take profit near $50,000.

Option two has several choices in terms of the type of B move; a regular flat and a zig zag would put the correction to around the $50,000 mark. But a running flat extension, which can often extend 123.6% of leg A, would put the upside level whilst still being a valid correction at $83,000 roughly.

The issue with the majority of retail traders is that they struggle to comprehend such a move; they see the price going up and assume it's only now bullish. Not just where the price goes, but how it gets there is a big factor that the majority overlook.

Option three meant a slow grind up and likely failure around the old high of $69,000 due to the lack of new liquidity.

Three images are worth seeing here.

Image from Chapter 18.

Think of the liquidity and where stops and entries are likely to be. The next image I share is from Chapter 20.

Longs versus shorts of the leveraged funds.

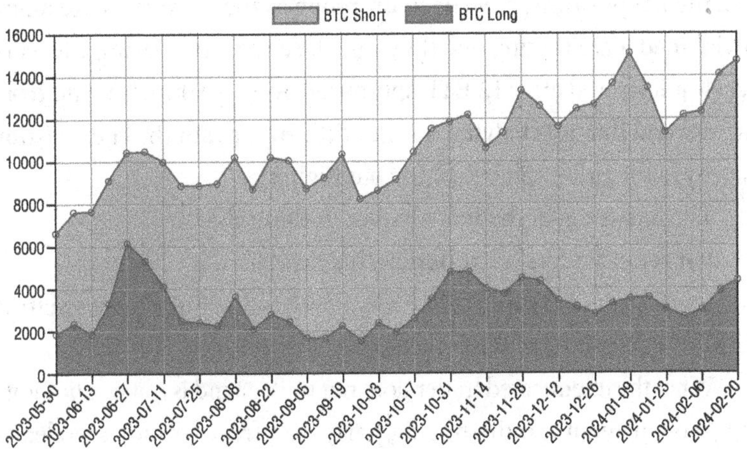

This last image shows the leveraged funds painted as an oscillator on the chart. Longs and shorts, but in addition there is a net position line. I have placed a line from its high to show the sell off.

The image shows COT as an oscillator.

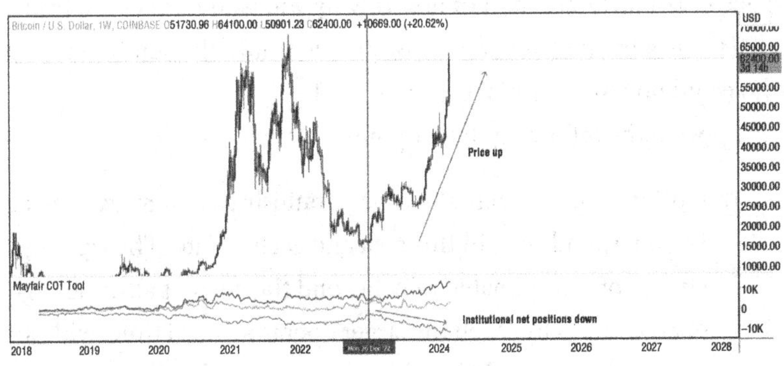

As the COT chart shows, the shorts are greater than the longs, and the net positions have been dropping as the price rises. Retail on social media are talking like they can't lose. We are nearing a level of vast liquidity and after 12 ETF approvals, over a year moving up from the low and Bitcoin's halving due in a little over a month. The question is, why is the price still below the old highs?

The answer is in the information in these charts.

For retail traders 'it's different this time'.

I hear people say things like 'COT is showing the big boys getting REKT' (a crypto term for recked).

What the uneducated trader does not understand is not one liquidity but two—if retail are the buying party—leveraged funds are clearly selling. The suggestion is they are willing to buy at a premium.

A classic example of wholesale selling to retail, just like the line outside an Apple store on launch day. Retail lines up to pay higher prices.

Like I said, this is part of the psychology: proper risk-to-reward management, which is part of how or why you would execute a trade.

This is a great example of how people think, the sentiment as a whole and how short-sighted people can be.

I posted the following three opinions.

1. Option one was actually a best, bullish case that would see Bitcoin spend time in this area and accumulate. Thus giving a chance of a sustainable rally beyond the current all-time high of $69,000. Why? Well the larger operators need time, without that time they would be paying a premium for the asset.
2. The second option of larger corrective (B) move meant that although we have moved up from $15,000 to currently near

the $65,000 mark, the price and attitude of the price movement do not have the hallmarks of an impulsive drive that will take price much beyond the current all-time high. People who are looking at 1-hour candles can't or don't seem to understand this as a possibility.

3. The third option was actually the worse case, although much like option one it was a bullish scenario. The issue is that it limits the upside.

Seeing the comments and the negativity because I have not said 'we can easily hit 100k, 250k or beyond' simply shows the naivety of the newer traders. For Composite Man, this is the easiest money to make.

When you zoom out to this kind of timeframe, the writing is on the wall. However, if you had wanted to use this information to your advantage to execute a trade, you could have looked at it and said that all three options point up from the low.

As we hit resistance at $32,000 regions, then broke through, option two would have been a stop loss below the resistance for an expected target 1 of $53,000 or beyond in the higher extension levels (trailing your stop loss).

Obviously the third option is also bullish, just capped at the triple top-type concept at the current all-time high of $69,000. It's how you use the data and logic in front of you that makes the difference.

What you have to remember is that, each trade setup is unique to you. Why you enter, where you enter, where you place your stop and take profit. I really like this Bitcoin example as it shows the lack of attention from people who watched part of a video, heard a negative Bitcoin word or two and left. This is what you call dumb money in the institutional world.

The assumption that something will continue up forever is exactly why deploying proper risk management and knowing your own entry and exit is crucial.

It would not be a surprise if we were to collect upside liquidity, not breach the all-time high by much and then start it's distribution schematic on the larger timeframe.

CHAPTER 29

PROP FIRMS

'It is difficult to get a man to understand something when his salary depends on his not understanding it.'

—John Kay

https://www.goodreads.com/quotes/7343290-it-is-difficult-to-get-a-man-to-understand-something

One more little thing I wanted to mention is that now you have these newfound skills, it's probably a good idea for you to do a little research into prop firm trading. The following is a good search definition of a prop firm.

A proprietary trading firm, often referred to as a 'prop firm' or 'prop trading firm', is a financial institution that engages in proprietary trading. Proprietary trading involves the firm trading its own money in the financial markets instead of executing trades on behalf of clients. Here are some key characteristics and aspects of prop trading firms:

Trading with Own Capital. Proprietary trading firms use their capital, rather than client funds, to engage in buying and selling financial instruments such as stocks, bonds, commodities, currencies and derivatives.

Profit Motive. The primary goal of a prop trading firm is to generate profits from market movements. Successful proprietary trading can result in financial gains for the firm.

Risk Management. Proprietary trading involves inherent risks, so these firms typically employ sophisticated risk management strategies. They use various risk management tools and techniques to control and mitigate the potential downside of trading activities.

Market Specialisation. Some prop trading firms specialise in specific markets or asset classes. For example, a firm might focus exclusively on equity trading, foreign exchange (forex), options or commodities.

High-Frequency Trading (HFT). Some prop firms, particularly those with advanced technology and algorithmic trading capabilities, may engage in HFT. This involves executing many trades at extremely high speeds to capitalise on minor price discrepancies.

Technology and Algorithms. Prop trading firms rely heavily on technology and algorithmic trading strategies. Sophisticated trading algorithms analyse market data, identify opportunities and execute orders at optimal prices.

Independence. Unlike traditional brokerage firms, prop trading firms typically do not take client orders or provide brokerage services to external clients. Their focus is on using their funds for trading activities.

Compensation Structure. Traders at prop firms are often compensated based on their trading performance. Profitable traders may receive a share of the profits they generate, and this compensation structure can be different from the salary-based model standard in traditional financial institutions.

Regulation. Depending on the jurisdiction, proprietary trading is subject to various regulatory frameworks. In some regions, prop trading firms may operate as registered investment firms or fall under specific regulatory guidelines.

Capital Requirements. Prop trading firms must maintain sufficient capital to support their trading activities and comply with regulatory requirements. The amount of capital can vary based on the size and risk profile of the firm.

It's important to note that the term 'prop firm' can encompass a wide range of institutions, from smaller firms with a niche focus to larger firms with diverse trading strategies. The industry has evolved over the years, and technological advancements have played a significant role in shaping the landscape of proprietary trading.

I wanted to finish on this because I believe trading is all about mitigating as much risk as possible. You can limit your risk even further, something I have discussed in several streams, and create a prop firm blueprint.

The idea is to leverage some of these firms to your advantage.

For example, some firms offer a $10,000 account.

To obtain this level of funding, you would typically pay $150 as an entry fee. You then pass one or two stages, usually requiring 8–10% profit gain in stage one and 4–5% profit gain in stage two.

Once you do this, you get your $150 fee back and access to trade a $10,000 account. The next step in my blueprint could be using the first payout to fund another account.

Often, prop firms do a profit split—some range from 50%, others go up to 90%; so, assuming a 10% profitable month on a $10,000 account would mean you could receive up to $900.

If you use this profit to purchase another account, maybe double the size, say $20,000, you might be expected to pay $200–$300 for this account. The same rules apply to the 8–10% and 4–5% gains roughly. But within a few months, you could be full-time trading with limited risk. Nothing stops you from starting with a $100,000 or even greater account size. The only thing is, you pay more for the entry ticket. Hence, this is why I would suggest starting with smaller ones. Get used to it, and get a feel for the platform and your new strategies.

Scale at your own pace.

This allows you to limit your risk, scale even with different companies and get to a point you are happy with before you leap into professional trading.

Here's a link to one of the companies I use.

https://shorturl.at/hBEQ4

Take it easy, stay safe and have fun.

Good luck with your trading!

FURTHER EDUCATION

Thanks so much for reading my book. You've reached the end, but it doesn't have to stop there! Join me in our Discord server Mayfair Method: https://discord.gg/5t3w47raHe

Trading can be lonely, and finding beneficial information online is often difficult amid the chaos. So we provide a safe place where traders can support each other in their daily trading journey, giving relevant, up-to-date, live information, where you can even reach out directly to me. I'm here to help.

We launched in 2020 during the pandemic, and the craze where people seemed more desperate than ever to invest their life savings in crypto/forex/stocks after losing their jobs and frantically trying to make a living from home. Most didn't have a clue what they were doing or where they could go to learn.

The issue was, most didn't want to learn. But trading is NOT a 'get-rich-quick' fix, as often promoted, and sadly many people have found this fact out the hard way—often losing everything.

Our community is a friendly place, where all who genuinely want to learn how to trade are welcome. So far, the Mayfair Method has helped thousands of people from all walks of life gain the skills and confidence to trade, from doctors to lawyers, pilots and plumbers from all around the globe.

In fact, I want to thank all our Discord members for their support and constant encouragement. I'm glad that I've been able to help so many on their journey. Here is what a few have said about our Discord server:

'I'm excited. It's like seeing the matrix for the first time—finding chaotic patterns.'

'I'm accusing Lewis of being the Composite Man.'

'This is the best write-up on crypto and altcoins I have ever seen.'

'You helped me save more than Geico ever could.'

'Being a psychiatric nurse, I can give you a professional opinion and say you are correct on your "Understanding the Traders' Psychology" diagram. That is comparable to the 5 Stages of Grief and Dying, also known as the 5 Stages of Death.'

'Thanks for the helpful tutorial on Gann. We hope it helps others learn something new. It's been featured in Editors' Picks.'

'A life-changing phone call, now starting to see the bigger picture.'

'Thanks for selling shovels during the gold rush.'

'I want to be like you one day. . . a HERO.'

'I thought Lewis was a sophisticated AI Bot, too good.'

'It's been a privilege to learn from the Mayfair Group. They have given next-level content and insane tools.'

'Yeah, the Composite Man put gremlins in Lewis's computer. They can't let him share all the secrets.'

'I guess Lewis knows his shit.'

'Talk about gold; surprisingly, Lewis was right again ;-).'

'In a nutshell, you covered all my questions. Ten years of learning, and you matched it in an hour.'

'This is the most intelligent analysis I have ever read.'

'You realise that the book recommendations and guidance have changed my life.'

'I found an expert with experience.'

'This man is the best analyst on TradingView.'

'One question for Lewis, well two actually:

1. Are you the composite operator?
2. If not, do you know him and have daily contact?'

'Lewis said in 5 minutes what some guy on YouTube took an hour and a half to try and break down.'

'I feel so lucky to have found this awesome gem of a trader.'

'It pains me to admit it, but you were 100% right.'

'Like there's a spy among us, Mayfair is a master of puppets.'

'Good one, like the Arabic proverb. Today, you are dripping honey.'

'Wow, so cool, Mayfair just commented on my post—I must be right.'

'I have listened to Lewis's last stream at least three times. How can I download them?'

'You're more than an expert.'

'I am sure I speak for many when I say you are "must-read" content.'

'It's a mental game training for me, not just in trading. It's helped me in everyday life as well.'

'Learning from the best.'

'You called this to a T so far, how?'

'I just copied your style. Thanks for the publications. Changed my whole business model.'

'Near perfect, the bit that wasn't was my own mistake. Thanks for everything.'

'Just want to say I'm so happy to be here; I feel like I found education equivalent to winning the lottery.'

'Thank you for sharing! I value your opinion more than that of one hundred popular influencers.'

'Man you are a Genius.'

'Actually graduated to my first 100k in one go trade last week. . . Thanks to you.'

'With Lewis, we learn about the dark side of the moon.'

'Probably the only legit thing you'll find in the crypto world.'

'Us mere mortals take a while to catch up with your logic.'

ABOUT THE AUTHOR

Lewis Daniels (better known in the trading community as Mayfair Ventures) has been trading from the age of fifteen after visiting New York's Wall Street on a school trip from his native Wales. He has been educating and mentoring students on the Mayfair Method since 2012, teaching advanced techniques and introducing students to the professional side of training.

Author of *Master the Art of Trading* (2023), originally written as a primer for his then 11-year-old son, Lewis wanted to make trading accessible to all. The book provides a quick, clear and easy roadmap to the world of trading, exploring the grand theories and behavioural economics underpinning the markets, from Elliott Wave Theory to Composite Man. It is a comprehensive and engaging guide, geared to help novice and established traders alike, equipping them with the skills, techniques and confidence to hit the ground running and to make an impact.

You can reach the author at mayfairventuresfx@gmail.com

INDEX